Pender County

Pender County

A History in the Voices of Its People

David W. Frederiksen

THE
History
PRESS

Published by The History Press
Charleston, SC 29403
www.historypress.net

Cover image: Picnic at Moore's Creek Revolutionary War Battleground, site of a decisive Patriot victory against Scottish Highlanders in the early morning hours of February 27, 1776. *Courtesy of the Pender County Library.*

First published 2006

Manufactured in the United States

ISBN-10 1.59629.147.8
ISBN-13 978.1.59629.147.8
Library of Congress Cataloging-in-Publication Data

Frederiksen, David.
Pender County : a history in the voices of its people / David Frederiksen.
p. cm.
ISBN-13: 978-1-54020-417-2
ISBN-10: 1-59629-147-8 (alk. paper)
1. Pender County (N.C.)--History. 2. Pender County (N.C.)--Biography. I.
Title.
F262.P37F74 2006
975.6'25--dc22
2006024625

Contents

Acknowledgements

I would like to thank Julie Lane Frederiksen, whose love and patience in support of this writer's life is a work of art beyond compare, and to Olivia, my little muse. Thank you Frederiksens, Wellses, Lanes and Austin-Lanes everywhere. For scholarship and expertise, a special thanks to Mike Taylor and staff at the Pender County Library, the Pender County Historical Society, Rose Peters and the Historical Society of Topsail Island, Dr. Charles Cornwell and Joseph Sheppard. For encouragement, Dr. James G. Simpson, Dr. David Ohashi, Mrs. Celia Rivenbark, Mr. David Ennis and Mrs. Bonnie Eksten. And to all who shared stories in this book: you have captured my heart and soul!

Introduction

Well before soil-caked hands and sturdy backs finish packing the harvest's last peanuts, corn and tobacco, people in Pender County, North Carolina, are already watching what the land holds next. Most areas offer little suspense: row after perfect row of green stems and tall stocks prevail, the sight of which can hypnotize. In other places not so dusty and vast—where fluted lamp poles, wide streets and shade trees make blue skies seem closer—the same grassy tracts forever hold various time-honored institutions: the courthouse, train depot or general store.

Suddenly, on the small paved lots—what used to be a bank here, a gas station there—the land propagates (as if by magic) wireless Internet connections, gourmet coffee and almond biscotti.

Here, people gather to tell stories beside red glazed walls and brushed metal. Men in blue-and-white-knit sport shirts and women in beach-themed blouses prop their elbows on tables and rest their chins atop hands shaped like teepees. Raised fingers accompany the mention of old state highways and abandoned buildings, while furrowed foreheads recollect long-forgotten dates. Reassuring *mhmms*, soft chatter and Satchmo compete with the shrill hiss of espresso that pierces the mocha-scented air like pins and needles.

Though very much has changed since its discovery during the early colonial period, the landscape of Pender County—its evolving nature and what it has come to sustain—reflects the spirit of the people who have come to inhabit it. Ultimately, the history of this community stands in its ability to reconcile itself with both the physical world and the events that have come to define its borders.

Whether about farming, teaching, painting, lawmaking or lawbreaking, the following stories show the heart's desire for self-expression and search for harmony amid sometimes colossal forces that can just as easily divide with thousands of miles between as unite nose to nose in the eye of a hurricane.

Introduction

The places and events interviewees remember—a schoolhouse, the county fair, barbering school, the battlefield—deliver equal doses of joy, sadness, laughter and despair. Separately, these stories allow us access to worlds that are not our own; combined, they teach us of the one we all have in common.

A Brief Note on Pender County's History

Named for Tarboro native and Confederate General William Dorsey Pender, Pender County was established by acts of the North Carolina General Assembly in 1875. At just over nine hundred square miles, Pender County—bound by the Atlantic Ocean along its easternmost edge—was once part of its southern neighbor New Hanover County, which was founded in 1729.

Since its organization, the region has enjoyed the opportunities for transportation and commerce offered by the 202-mile Cape Fear River, the longest river entirely within the boundaries of North Carolina. Located in the coastal plains section of the state with ten townships, Pender County has a population of 41,000. Naval stores—tar, pitch, turpentine and the timber from which all were extracted—undergirded the region's early prosperity.

The eastern part of the county comprises several small barrier islands, including the beach town of Topsail Island, once home to Operation Bumblebee, a top-secret U.S. Navy missile program. Central and western parts of the county are mainly rural with swampland interspersed.

With its name from Native American origin, Burgaw first appeared in land grants as early as 1728. The city was established as the county seat in the spring of 1879, moving from its previous location of nearby South Washington.

Pender County is home to the Burgaw Depot (1850), a product of the Wilmington and Weldon Railroad, and Sloop Point Plantation (1726), believed to be North Carolina's oldest house. Today, farming, small businesses, some industry and tourism make up the county's economic base.

How the Story Ends: Adline Johnson

You can't grow up with a whole lot of hate—that will destroy you.

We had briefly spoken the night before, and she agreed to meet me at the Pender County library to talk. I first saw her standing near a bookrack, her wide eyes behind voluminous glasses fixed on various titles with yellow dog-eared pages. In her bright pink blouse she looked like she'd just risen up out of an azalea bush, an impressive woman with curly gray hair and chocolate brown skin.

Through a big picture window behind her, the morning light gently stroked her back, while shadows from green trees with tiny new tendrils washed over her feet. Shifting her weight back and forth over powerful legs in brown hose with a giant sagging purse in one hand and a book held high in the other, Adline shooed gravity like a fly.

There was little formal introduction. She said she had just come from gardening. I pointed the way to a small conference room. Sitting down, she asked my name again and wrote it in big cursive letters in a small blue notebook.

Born in Little Kelly, an area just a few miles outside Burgaw, Adline Johnson had twelve brothers and sisters. Her father died when she was eight years old. Left to fend for themselves, the family picked cotton, cleared land and washed clothes in the homes of whites nearby. What little education she received took place in a one-room schoolhouse with books whose stories had no endings because of missing pages. It was a life she described as "terrible hard."

My hometown is Little Kelly. It's about seven miles from Burgaw. There's two Kellys—Big Kelly and Little Kelly. The school is still there but it's in disrepair. The grades ran from first grade through fifth or sixth grade. The school had one teacher.

Life at school was tough. In the wintertime we had to go into the woods and get our own firewood. Now and then the board of education would give us some coal—all the other schools had coal. Our school was just a little one-room run-down school with all these kids in it. We had fun, though.

When we got our books from the board of education, half the pages would be torn out. If we started a story, we could never end it because the pages were torn out. Even when we enrolled in other schools, we still got books with half the pages torn out. The school was leaking, and we had to put pails out to catch the rainwater from the roof. It was horrible, but through all of this we learned something.

When school would close in the summer, we would have little recitals at the school and our parents would bring lunch. We'd spread it out and have a picnic and have lots of fun. But we didn't get to learn the most important things because we didn't have the books. They would never give us good books. They would never furnish our schools (like the other schools were furnished) so we could get a good education. We would have to start our fires in the morning, and in the afternoon the boys would have to go back into the woods in order to get wood for the next day's fire. We always wondered, "Why, why was all this happening to us? Why were the black schools not being treated fairly?"

Was it because they didn't want us to get an education, because they thought if a black person got an education, then they could use it to better their lives? They would cancel school a lot of times, so you could go help the white man on the farm. I guess they figured if you didn't learn too much, then you couldn't do anything for yourself. This was in the 1930s, 1940s and 1950s.

You were free labor—know what I mean? You wasn't expected to get nowhere in life. And you wasn't expected to make too much money. The white man thought if you made any money, you'd get too high up on the ladder. This is how people kept you down: they worked you hard. Many times when we sharecropped in the fields at the end of the year, the man would tell my mother, "Well, you didn't make no money, and neither did I." We knew that he lied. He had kept all the money. As we grew up, we figured the man mistreated our mother, but she always said there would be a better day. We didn't know when, but we wanted to know when because it was so tough for us. You worked out in the field all day from sunup to sundown for a year through wintertime. You helped clear land and cut trees for farming, and then you'd take a grubbing hoe and shovel and dig up the land just like a person in a bulldozer. You would dig it up so they could farm it. You were never out of a job.

We were always wondering, "When, when was it going to change?" You worked a whole year, and you didn't have anything even to buy groceries with. You don't have any money to take care of your family with. We lived by the mercy of God. We survived because we knew how to work. We could take a hoe and almost make a farm. We had ten acres of land of our own. You could make sweet potatoes and all kinds of vegetables, and then you could have chickens and pigs. If the sow had too many pigs, my mother would take some of the pigs and put them in a box and nurse them up. We had a mule one time, and he got sick and couldn't get up. My mother went and got some esetica and baking soda and put it together and put it in a bottle, and she kept holding the mule's mouth open. She would take baking soda, put it in warm water and let it dissolve, and she would go in that mule's stable and open that mule's mouth and pour just as much as he could swallow in there. She would do that for a few days. And in three days the mule would be standing up, ready to plow again.

All this work and mistreatment made you angry and built you up and made you stronger in mind and your thinking and your doing for this present day. But I don't like to think back too much because you get those negative feelings. I never taught my kids to hate because my mother never taught us to hate. What my mother raised us on was the Bible in one hand and discipline in the other. When we would be crying in the field and things didn't go right, she would take her apron and wipe our face and say, "Baby, it's going to be OK after awhile…things are going to change after awhile…things are going to be OK." But it never did. Even when my kids came along, it hadn't changed too much.

Little Kelly school class picture. Date unknown. *Courtesy of Mrs. Adline Johnson.*

I learned to plow with a mule when I was about twelve. Every time one of us children got old enough we had to learn to plow. The first time I plowed I held the handles, and my brother would hold the lines. And we would get to the end of the row, he'd turn the mule around and we'd go back down the next row. My mother took in washing for a dollar a day. And then she would iron all the clothes for fifty cents. That was a dollar fifty for washing and ironing.

I remember the first time she let me go help other people. I was about fourteen. I helped this lady with her children. We could go work like that and make some money, maybe fifty cents or seventy-five cents. So there was a way that you could survive. We didn't have all this stuff you have now. You could take brown peas, you could cook them without any grease and you could eat them because you knew you didn't have anything else to eat. You could survive on most anything. I remember my mother cooking soybeans a lot of times. Sometimes she had something to go in them (maybe a little piece of fatback) and sometimes she wouldn't. We would eat whatever because we knew that we had to eat. We learned to be thankful and grateful to God for anything.

When my mother would wash at people's houses, they would give her old clothes. And she would take those clothes, and she could take a brown paper bag—anything to make a pattern—and she would make us clothes. I wore men's shoes to school. On many a day, if the sole was coming off she would take a piece of wire and connect it back together onto the shoe, and we would wear them to school.

Of course, we'd get picked at and laughed at, but it was always okay because she always said it was going to be a better day. She would make all our underclothes and everything we wore. We might not look like the other children, but still we were clean. We'd come home from school and we'd pull our clothes off and wash them, and we'd hang them up outside until it got dark. And then we'd bring them in the house and put them behind the wood heater and let them get dry. We'd put them on the next day and wear them again. The most important thing is that you were clean and you were getting an education. It wasn't what you had that mattered, it was getting an education. Of course, some black people had stuff, and then some didn't and some were at the bottom of the barrel. I guess you would call us at the bottom of the barrel.

My mother taught us so many valuable things: it's not what you have, it's really your heart—how you feel. You can't grow up with a whole lot of hate—that will destroy you. You got to grow up with being thankful, especially for who you are. Don't try to be somebody that you are not because that will destroy you too.

Native Progress:
Charles Harrell

I feel that when you're in a small town, or a town of any size, that you need to give back to the community in some way...

My chuckling began over the contents of a small white box at Harrell's Department Store in downtown Burgaw across from the courthouse. Amid a bin of carefully arranged men's dress shirts appeared half a dozen black shirt garters. "A few men still ask for them," said a pleasant woman behind a glass counter holding a huge plastic mug, the kind you find at a 7-Eleven.

That a device of such small detail might still be found in an era where shirttails go deliberately untucked confirmed the legacy of this 103-year-old department store and the fondness of third-generation owner Charles Harrell for the unconventional.

Well over six feet tall with gray wavy hair and deep-set eyes, Mr. Harrell was born in Pender County and served six terms as mayor of Burgaw from 1969 to 1971 and again from 1977 to 1987. He spent his childhood in and out of the Dry Goods and Notions store his grandfather built at the turn of the century before serving in the Pacific in World War II. His involvement in establishing a local chapter of the Jaycees and other civic and economic organizations in Pender County helped introduce new industries in an area largely possessed of small family farms.

Dressed in a beige button-down shirt, purple tie and tweed sport coat, Mr. Harrell emerged from a corner of the store near the glass storefront where the morning light was just beginning to creep. His eyes steady on the courthouse beyond, he lowered himself onto a wooden chair and, pointing to reddish-brown photographs of people and buildings behind him, began to speak.

Native Progress: Charles Harrell

My grandfather lost a leg when he was fourteen years old from an accident. He told me they held him down on a table and cut his leg off. No anesthesia. He became a farmer and moved from Sheridan Crossroads up in Duplin County to Pender in 1890. He farmed for a little while and then moved into Burgaw in 1901 or 1902 and went into business and built the building next to us.

The town of Burgaw was laid out by engineers from the railroad—we don't have a First, Second or Third Street. All of our streets have names like Dickerson Street, Wright Street and Cowan Street. I understand all of these names were railroad names: presidents, vice-presidents and so on. Burgaw was a railroad town. In fact, they called it Burgaw Depot for a while.

I was instrumental in saving the train depot. A lot of people wanted to destroy it and get rid of it. I felt that we should keep the depot. They also wanted to get rid of the jail, but this is the fabric and integrity of this area. When the coastline abandoned this part of the railroad—they disconnected the railroad at Castle Hayne where the bridge is—the depot was sort of neglected. We tried to save the depot and get it refurbished. We put a new roof on it a couple of times. So we're right now working on a program to do more to the depot. This is one of North Carolina's oldest depots, and it burned at one time. Charred timbers are still in there.

As far back as I can remember, we had crank telephones on the wall and they were owned by Mr. and Mrs. J.D. Waddell. It was the Pender Telephone Company. They had a few rural lines but the phones were mostly in town. She ran the phone company out of her home in a central office in the front room of her house. She had the switchboard there. When the Jaycees organized, one of our projects was to get better phone service in Burgaw. Mrs. Waddell didn't appreciate that, but sold out to Southern Bell. They had to take out her whole system. They had to bring all new equipment and all new lines. Mrs. Waddell was sort of peeved; we knew the phone system was holding us back.

My daddy was very instrumental in putting in the original water and sewer in Burgaw because I remember when the ditches were open along these streets. Before that, we just had johns and home water systems. My father put a water system in our backyard to serve five houses besides ours—this was before the town water system.

W.R. Harrell's store, Dry Goods and Notions, circa 1915. This later became Harrell's Department Store. *Courtesy of the Pender County Musuem.*

I first went in office as commissioner in 1953. I was asked to take the place of a person who was dying. After six months of service, he resigned, so I took the year-and-a-half remaining time, and then I ran for office subsequent to that. Then I became mayor for six terms, and I'm back on the board of commissioners now. I feel that when you're in a small town, or a town of any size, that you need to give back to the community in some way, whether it's through the church or in civic duties. Pender County's been good to us for 103 years.

Of course, we were always working on economic development. We donated my daddy's old cow pasture over in the northern part of the town for the W.R. Harrell Memorial Park. In those days, a lot of people had cows in their backyard. That was the area that daddy had a cow pasture, and we put the cows out during the day and we—my family, my siblings and I—donated that land and started the W.R. Harrell Memorial Park, which is over on Walker Street next to the courthouse. We started the Pender Progress Corporation, which was an industrial development group, and we bought sixty-eight acres just down behind the schoolhouse here and put in water, sewer and streets and sold that off for industry. We sold it at a very reasonable price. Then we bought an additional forty-five or fifty acres and developed that. I'm still involved in that. So that was one of our projects when I was mayor.

Built in 1850, the Burgaw Depot, originally on the Wilmington and Weldon line, is one of the oldest depots in the state. *Courtesy of the Pender County Library.*

In those days we didn't have town managers, so the mayor did all the hiring and firing and general management of the town. We had a public works superintendent. But we were always pushing to get industry in. We took a group and went to Buffalo, New York. Twelve of us went during December, and we stayed in the motel at the airport and rented cars. Two of us would go out together, and we had our designated places to go see if they would be interested in expanding their operations in our area. It was a good experience and we were treated very, very nicely. We went to one place, Mosler Heat Reduction Units—those are little units where people use a volume of water and have to cool it off and reuse it. They made heat reduction units from small to large. Some were so huge they had to be manufactured outdoors. When I called Mosler that morning, he said, "Well, I've got about twenty to twenty-five minutes I can give you." We just called him cold turkey, and we ended up staying with him for three hours.

Portrait of a Young Lawyer: Clifton L. Moore Jr.

Son, if they had wanted to do anything to us or harm us, they could have done it. They were just trying to frighten and intimidate us.

Clifton Moore Jr. was already halfway into a story before I could finish "hello." After a quick handshake on the front steps of his brick home not far from downtown Burgaw, the tall lean-bodied figure in gray trousers and white shirt—a lawyer by profession—led the way to a room with a TV and big picture window. A worn oriental rug muffled our footsteps, and we settled into two big wingback chairs—his burgundy, mine mustard yellow—and spoke of spring pollen and cures for achy sinuses.

High above Cliff was a picture of two small children a few years apart with red hair and fair skin. I tried hard to date the color portrait—whether his children or grandchildren—but gave up in favor of imagining freckled faces watching television with milk and cookies in hand. On a nearby secretary, a miniature gnome with a playful grin looked across at us.

In the dining room, a portrait of Cliff's father, Judge Clifton L. Moore Sr., in a dark business suit and tie revealed features immediately familiar in the face of my new host: the long, square face with ears back set slightly below snow-white hair. His smile was gentle, fitting for a man of few words and slow to anger, as Cliff would say later.

In 1952, as solicitor of nearby Columbus County, Judge Moore successfully prosecuted more than ninety-three Klansmen, ending a significant reign of terror by the Ku Klux Klan. Soon after, Judge Moore urged passing of the Moore Act, which to this day outlaws secret political and military organizations in the state.

Portrait of a Young Lawyer: Clifton L. Moore Jr.

In the narrative below, Cliff Jr. reflects on the courtroom atmosphere during the trial and on two events in particular that would come to teach the future lawyer and Burgaw mayor (1971–1973) the full impact of his father's work in an era of rapid social change.

I was just a teenager then and had gone to pick my father up from the trial in Whiteville. I think the judge's name was Clawson Williams. I can picture it right now. It was your typical courthouse and courtroom like we have here in Burgaw, an old-timey kind with a second floor and big windows. My father had not talked much about the Klan's activities to me or the rest of the family—I'd picked up little things here and there. But of course it had been in the papers and everybody knew about it. I was old enough to go in and watch some of the trial. I had never been in anything like that before or seen anything like that before. And I don't really believe I've ever been involved in anything that was quite as tense since then.

The courtroom was full of law officers, highway patrolmen, town police, deputy sheriffs and State Bureau of Investigation (SBI) agents. They were lined up around the walls—being sixteen years old, that impressed me—and, of course, when the people came into the courtroom, they closed the doors and they were locked.

My recollection is that when you went in you had to sit down and put your hands up on the back of the chair in front of you. The court instructed everybody not to get up and not to leave until they called a recess. Of course I sat down and heard some of the trial. I was impressed by the security of it. Now you've got to remember this was back when they didn't have cameras in the courtroom. Maybe one or two bailiffs were all you ever had. It was just so unusual and stressful. It was a situation I had never been in before. Of course, when they recessed, I didn't go back in there.

We had just left Whiteville and started home. There's a stretch of highway that runs from White Lake through Pender County. My father was driving. It wasn't a heavily trafficked road. It was a lonesome road. There weren't any vehicles on it, and there were no homes out there. He was driving, and we were riding along, and after we'd been traveling for a while, he got real quiet.

Judge Clifton L. Moore Sr. *Courtesy of the Pender County Musuem.*

Finally, he said something to the effect of, "Now, Son, don't get upset, but somebody has been following us ever since we left Whiteville." And naturally I turned around and looked. I could see a vehicle with lights that were big—it had gotten dark—at some distance behind us. I don't know what conversation my father and I had at that point. I probably questioned him how he knew that we were being followed. At any rate, we were going along and this car came up behind us, and we were right there in this totally desolate area. The car came up, and I could tell by looking at the vehicle that it probably had five men in it and I'm sure they could have been dangerous. I don't know why I have in my mind that it was a taxicab. It came up on us and suddenly they passed us—just like anybody would pass—they picked up speed and just passed. And they went on down the road. As they got a pretty good little distance ahead of us, they pulled over and they didn't come to a dead stop.

They pulled over and they pulled out into the road. My recollection is that that the car wasn't all the way across the road, but I'd say it was a little bit over the center line. As I said earlier, my father had on prior occasions been threatened by the Klan, which I had been aware of. He was the prosecutor in the case. It was just a tense sort of situation. My father just kept on going. We were in a black straight-shift Chevrolet automobile. As my father started up the road, the nearer he got to them, the faster he went. And when he got right near them, right to them, he just went around them. He went off of the road—I remember that. And just as he got straightened back out on the highway, they cranked up and fell in behind us again. They followed us to this small town on the edge of Pender County called Atkinson.

We were just getting into the outskirts of Atkinson, and they slowed down and turned around. Father said, "Son, if they had wanted to do anything to us or harm us, they could have done it. They were just trying to frighten and intimidate us."

One evening we were just sitting, watching the ballgame—there was nobody else here but us—and the phone rang. My father went to the phone and came back out here and sat back in his chair for a few minutes. Then he got up and went into the closet in the hall, and he got his double-barrel shotgun and a box of shells. And he came back in and sat down and put the gun in the corner.

He just sat back down. He didn't say anything. It certainly wasn't a "garden variety" kind of thing to be seeing. I said, "Well, Father, what in the world are you doing?" He said, "Well, Son, I just got a call and there's a rumor that the Klan's going to 'wait on' J.K. Powell" (he was assisting Father) "and Mr. Powell said they were going to wait on him, and then they were going to come wait on me." I said, "Don't you think you need to go call Chief Ward, the chief of police?" He said, "No, I don't think they're coming, but the only way this is going to stop from happening is when they go to somebody's house one night and somebody really gets hurt. Somebody's going to have to leave one or some of them lying in the yard, and if they come here tonight, that may happen."

A Place for All Things:
Mary Bowen Caputo

Everybody else I've ever heard of who had an ancestor during the Civil War claimed he was a general, never less than a colonel. I have proof my grandfather was a private.

When Mary Bowen Caputo lands her long champagne-colored Cadillac in the gravel lot in front of the Pender County Museum on West Bridgers Street, she brings in tow a lifetime of experiences many of us only dream about: journalist, world traveler, diplomat's wife.

On a day that felt more like mid-July than early April, Mrs. Bowen appeared dressed in a blue blouse and white slacks with a sharp crease. Rising gently from the driver's seat amid a swirl of dust at her feet, she walked gracefully and purposefully to the museum door, a bag in each hand.

"We must not forget to sign the register," she said, smiling, as we entered the two-story brick building that housed the Pender County Historical Society's collections. As I signed my name, I could see in the margins of sheets before mine beginnings of the letter M, which I took to be Mary's. Upon later inspection I would come to find her signature repeated countless times, each reassuringly the same. The evenness and uniformity of her letters, huddled close together without sacrificing clarity, suggested she was someone who knew how to be part of a group but also treasured individuality.

We sat opposite one another and rested our elbows on a long brown banquet table. To my front, wall shelves featured fuzzy photographs of pioneer men, women and children, their faces stiff and scared. On other shelves, porcelain dolls in bows and long flowing dresses pointed with chipped and worn fingers. Rooms elsewhere contained vintage clothing, the occasional chaise lounge or end table and, in one dark display case, a limp-looking gas mask so old it seemed to gasp for air.

Born and raised in Pender County, Mrs. Bowen returned again and again when war took her husband, a career marine, overseas. Mary discussed her life, the beginnings of the Pender County Historical Society and Museum and some of the county's earliest families.

I grew up here with lots of cousins. Within a year after my graduation from the University of North Carolina at Chapel Hill School of Journalism, my career as a newspaper reporter was cut short when I married a marine. My husband was in the Marine Corps for almost thirty years, and I found that every time he went to war—World War II, Korea, Vietnam—I came back to Burgaw, so I never lost contact with Burgaw.

After Tony retired from the Marine Corps, he went into business for about twelve years. We were living in Atlanta, and I thought we really needed to put down roots. Our children were both grown and had finished college and the more we thought about it, the more we thought Burgaw was the place for us. Of all the places that we've ever lived—Sweden, Hawaii, the East Coast and the West Coast—we decided Burgaw suited us better than anyplace else.

I grew up on my grandfather's estate. As I said, I had a lot of cousins. We all lived in the same neighborhood. My grandfather built the original house around 1880. Two of his sons built to the east of that house and two sons to the west, and there were twenty-three first cousins living there, surrounding the old homeplace.

I had in all forty-seven first cousins. It was a large family, an interesting family. Everybody in the family liked to talk. Three of the brothers—my uncles—had moved to Florida in the 1920s, and they would come back frequently to visit, and I can remember evenings sitting on the front porch in rocking chairs and hearing the older people talk. When I was growing up, children really were seen and not heard, but I learned a lot because I listened to all these tales.

The oldest member of that family would come up and visit and talk incessantly, but the stories he told were absolutely wonderful.

An evangelist spreads the Word. *Courtesy of the Pender County Library.*

One of the things that they talked about was religion. Those were the days when radio was in its infancy. There was no television, of course, no movies in this area, and one of the big entertainments was church.

The three main churches—Baptist, Presbyterian and Methodist—had revivals every year, and they would invite a visiting minister to come and give a series of sermons. Many of them had both morning and evening services—and this doesn't sound very nice—but it was really more entertainment. One year the Presbyterian Church had invited a visiting evangelist, and his reputation spread so rapidly that he was a dynamic speaker. The church could no longer hold the congregation and they had to move to the high school auditorium, which was enormous, and it was filled pretty much. This was in the days when they preached hellfire and damnation. And this man, I think, was the champion of all.

I have so many warm memories of growing up with all these cousins and friends in town. Of course, those were the days when children could skate on the courthouse square. The courthouse that preceded the present one had just one step up from the sidewalk, and it had marble floors. And I can remember well as a child we could skate up to the front door, jump up and skate all the way through and out the back door. And nobody ever chastised us. We never caused any harm. We never bothered anybody. It's just the way it was.

We could skate to the stores downtown. Children behaved in a small town. Everybody knew everybody's children. No one there misbehaved much because if they did anything mischievous, before they could get home the word had already gotten to their parents. Everybody sort of looked out for everybody else. Those were the days when front porches were in vogue. There was no air conditioning—nobody was inside watching soap operas. In the afternoons all the ladies would sit on the front porch and watch the children playing on the sidewalk. People visited a lot and it was a very warm community.

[These were] the days when my father was clerk of court, and if after school I stayed to skate my father would give me a nickel and I could go to the grocery store and treat all my friends. And if Father were out of the office, I would go to the grocery store and charge a nickel's worth of candy to his account.

I also knew a Confederate veteran from the Civil War. He sat on his front porch. His house is still standing on Walker Street in Burgaw. I remember many, many times as a child—I had friends who lived in that neighborhood—and this was old Mr. T.J. Bradshaw, and he sat on his porch all summer. And we were often playing in the neighborhood and would always speak to him and he would wave to us. I never had a long conversation with him. (As a matter of fact, his grandson died the day before yesterday.) Mr. Bradshaw had a white beard; he was tall and thin and just a very nice man. He was always in church every Sunday. He had a large family. His first wife died. I think they had three children. We have a picture of Mr. Bradshaw and his second wife with all the children.

My grandfather was a Civil War veteran who died before I was born. Many people say, "No, that can't be, it must have been your great-grandfather," but it was not. It was my grandfather. And he's the first person I'm going to see when I get to heaven.

The Pender County Historical Society was formed in 1951. It became inactive for a few years and then came back to life in 1971

29

John Player Bannerman
27 June 1811-24 Oct. 1887

John Player Bannerman (1811–1887), builder and owner of the Bannerman home. *Courtesy of the Pender County Museum.*

with people who were interested in preserving local history. In 1975 Pender County celebrated its one hundredth anniversary, and that brought out a lot of things that nobody had thought about before.

Every community in Pender County had a day that it was featured. They had a big celebration. All of the local people brought out everything that they could think of that could be of interest and that sparked the idea that we needed a museum. Papers, clothes, deeds, letters, artifacts of every kind had been tucked away in a closet or trunk somewhere, but when each community celebrated its day, these things were brought out. And everybody was interested in them.

Then in 1979, Burgaw celebrated its one hundredth anniversary and the same thing happened. The opportunity presented itself when two lovely kind ladies who had grown up in this house, which is now the Pender County Museum (they had been school teachers), were no longer able to travel between Burgaw and Florida and wanted to get rid of this house. We suggested that perhaps they would like to donate their home for a museum, which they did. So the Pender County Historical Society was very fortunate in obtaining this place. This has been my main interest ever since the museum was opened in December of 1979.

A Place for All Things: Mary Bowen Caputo

Original Bannerman house, date unknown. *Courtesy of the Pender County Library.*

My interest also is in genealogy, and I was able to get a lot of information about my grandfather who was, as I claim, the "only enlisted man in the Confederate States Army." Everybody else I've ever heard of who had an ancestor during the Civil War claimed he was a general, never less than a colonel. I have proof my grandfather was a private. So I think that is really a great claim to fame if he was the only one. I have muster rolls showing that he was slightly wounded and captured at Spotsylvania on May 12, 1864, and sent to Elmira, New York, as a prisoner of war. I have done a lot of research. I have been to Elmira. I've done a lot of reading and visiting cemeteries and courthouses to get as many facts as I can. I have written a book about my family mainly because of my interest in my grandfather.

One of the things that's impressed me most is that there have been two families who have long, long histories connected with Pender County—of course, it was New Hanover County until 1875—but these two families have given the Pender County Museum the majority of the valuable artifacts that we own. Those two families are the Bannerman family and the Armstrong family from Rocky Point. We've been given old newspapers, some dating as far back as 1858. I think one of the earliest of the local papers dates to 1889. And these are just intriguing to

In Pender County's early days, children died of common diseases. *Courtesy of the Carrie Rowe Collection, Pender County Library.*

read. It's amazing to see the difference in style. It's just delightful to read some of the early accounts—very flowery language, very descriptive—and when you read an article, particularly about a wedding or a party, you feel as though you've been there. Today, things are cut and dried. We don't go into nearly as much description. But these things are delightful. Nowadays, no one has time to write that kind of thing or to read it.

The Bannermans were a very prominent family. They lived in an area called Bannermans. They had a post office, as did most communities, and later it was called Bannerman's Bridge. They had a very large plantation…One of the things we were given from that family is the family bible which records not only all the statistics about the family but also about the slaves, which is an unusual thing to find these days. They gave us an original land grant dated in the "nineteenth year of our independence and in the year of our Lord one thousand seven hundred ninety-four."

The Armstrong family from Rocky Point was very prominent. There are so many people in that family named T.J. Armstrong—I don't know how many generations there were. The only one I can remember was called T.J. Armstrong Jr., but he was at least the fourth member of that family by that name. We have his diploma from the University of North Carolina, class of 1909.

A Place for All Things: Mary Bowen Caputo

Both families were big landowners and had rather large families and were prominent also in civic life, if you can call county life civic. They were well educated, very helpful as far as schools and that type of thing—just good, honest people. Unfortunately, both of those families died out, there are no direct descendents left. The last direct descendent of the Bannerman family died about six years ago, but he and his wife had given the museum the majority of the really fine artifacts that we have here: papers, deeds, letters, some Civil War letters, the land grant I mentioned earlier, everything imaginable. The Armstrongs gave us a lot of furniture. That was given by the foster son of T.J. Armstrong "Jr." (I put "Jr." in quotes because he was way down the line, but he was the one who graduated from Carolina in 1909.) His foster son gave us a pistol that had been given to a little Armstrong boy. The little boy had led a group of Confederate soldiers around a Union encampment, and in that way prevented their capture and possibly saved their lives. In appreciation an officer gave this pistol to the little boy.

In both cases children died at very early ages. We have from each of those families a tea set from the Armstrong family and a silver cup from the Bannerman family. Both belonged to little girls who only lived ten years. When I was telling a group of young schoolchildren about this, I said this tea set belonged to a little girl who only lived to be ten years old. The question from one of the young schoolchildren was, "Who shot her?" Children are not aware that youngsters used to die of the common diseases that all children had. But now there are inoculations against them, and it's rare to hear of children dying at that age unless they are in an accident. But children today think if a child dies they were either killed in an automobile accident or they were shot. If you go into old cemeteries you can often find seven, eight or nine infant graves from the same family ranging from children who were still born or died by the time they were two or three years old. There was one family in what is now Pender County who had five children who died within six weeks from what I think was diphtheria. That was back before 1900.

BOLO:
Mike Bell

In my career I have probably worked 130 to 140 escapes, and this was one of those handful that I had an uneasy feeling about.

Three ballpoint pens made of fine wood with brass clips encased in a wood and glass box with velvet lining first caught my eye when I entered Mike Bell's office.

As chief correctional administrator at the Pender Correctional Institution located on Penderlea Highway just a few miles from the courthouse, Harrell's and the museum, Mike supervises over 750 medium-security inmates, some of them with life sentences. As such, the facility (with a history dating to the 1930s) ranks as one of the larger industries in Pender County, employing hundreds of nearby residents and infusing millions of dollars into the local economy.

In an office built of cinder blocks painted soft yellow with a single window positioned curiously high, Mike spoke about the history of the North Carolina prison system, a system that began, he said, in the aftermath of the Civil War.

Pender County became part of this history in 1935 when a one-dormitory barn-like prison was built. It was one of sixty-one original field unit prisons constructed statewide during the 1930s to house inmates who worked building roads.

As Mike turned to show me an aerial photograph of the old drafty facility, a snow-covered mountain seemed to tear from its canvas and become part of the surrounding cement, while three prowling tigers in separate frames on another wall peered through bamboo as if to join us.

I glanced again at the pens on Mike's desk. They were so official-looking: Were they solely decorative? Did they hold the ink that gave men their freedom? If so, what were the men like?

BOLO: Mike Bell

These questions would have to wait, as I turned my ears to Mike's deep Southern drawl for more information on Pender's prison history and a near escape that began one cold January night years ago.

We have a long history: our central prison in Raleigh was built back in the 1880s as a condition of North Carolina reentering the Union after the Civil War. I think the Federal government required that all Southern states (as a condition of getting back into the Union) had to build a central prison. Typically, central prisons are in your capital cities. We have a unique system in North Carolina in that we have seventy-seven prisons. Most states have far fewer prisons, but they're megaprisons with thousands of inmates.

Back in the early days of our correctional system, each county had what they called a county farm. The highway department and the prison department were sort of merged because the emphasis back in those days was working the roads. That's why whenever you travel across North Carolina and you see prisons, you will typically see a department of transportation facility right next door. That's the way it is here in Pender County. The original prison here was built back in the 1930s. A lot of these prisons were built during the same period of time.

As you travel around the state, you will see the same kind of architecture in all those original prisons that were built under the old WPA days during the Roosevelt administration. The architecture is almost identical—a long rectangular building. You would have a little small area in the center where the correctional officer, a guard (as they were called back in the early days) stayed. Those old prisons would typically have two large dormitories, one on each side, and in the center there would be a caged-in area where the officer would patrol. The dorms were open bay. It would house about sixty-five to seventy on each side. A lot of people have the misconception that all prisons are single-cell, but very few prisons are single-cell. Most of the prisons are dormitory style where you have as many as sixty or seventy inmates living in the same area like a military barrack.

The emphasis in the early days was working the highways. They had chain gangs. They used to have these cages or trailers that they would hook behind the DOT trucks, and they would pull the trailers to wherever the work site was. Typically, they were benches with hooks in the floor where they could hook the shackles. And they were not enclosed—they had tarps that would roll down on the sides of the trailer.

This prison here was one of those road camps, originally. Of course, over the years many of those have been closed down. And as we modernized and built new prisons, those old structures lost a lot of their usefulness.

Our old original prison here was converted into a sewing factory when this prison expanded in the early 1990s. This prison up until the early 1990s only held about 130 inmates in that single-dormitory structure. When we expanded into the 768 we have here, we converted that old prison into part of a sewing factory for what we call correctional enterprise.

The last escape attempt was an inmate coming back from court under the supervision of a deputy sheriff, and they pulled up to that stop sign right out there. The deputy had known the prisoner for years. He had him in the front seat only with a pair of handcuffs, and the inmate got to that stop sign and looked over here at this prison and said, "I ain't going back."

And he reached over and took the deputy's pistol away from him. He told the deputy to drive. The deputy put the car in the ditch. The inmate pointed the gun at him and pulled the trigger, but the gun was on safe. The deputy rolled out of the vehicle. And the inmate got in the driver's seat and drove down Penderlea Road to escape. He had the deputy's coat, hat, his weapon and his car. He had somehow gotten one hand out of one side of the cuffs. We searched for him all night long.

It was a cold January night a few years ago. I had gone home. The inmate had gone to Carteret County and had gotten an additional sentence—it wasn't but a couple years added on—and that was a scary night. Once he escaped, we went into full mobilization. They called me. I immediately came back. We notified highway patrol, Pender County Sheriff's Department, the Burgaw Police Department. We started our process of trying to figure out where this guy went. Of course, he was in a marked car. The highway patrol sent out a bulletin, a BOLO: Be-On-Look-Out for. He was not spotted, so that led us to the conclusion that instead of trying to get away at a high rate of speed and put as much distance between him and us, he's held up somewhere.

We had already mobilized our staff. We have what's known as a PERT team—Prison Emergency Response Team. These folks have special training for prison emergencies, and of course this would have fallen under the category of prison emergency: you got an armed felon who's pulled the trigger and would have tried to kill the deputy and [stolen] his gun, and he's on the loose in our community. We were searching back roads all the way from here down to Penderlea. We had all available staff on it, and other law enforcement was assisting us.

We got some intelligence that this inmate had a friend in Castle Hayne. So we made contact with that friend and said, "Have you heard from so and so?" He said, "Well, I guarantee you that if he's escaped he's going to contact me." We got him to agree that he would let us know. Of course, we staked out that neighborhood.

As it turns out, we found out the next morning the inmate had gone several miles down the road and had put that police car way back up in the woods and had basically just sat there. He said he saw us flashing our spotlights into the woods.

Somewhere around three or four o'clock in the morning the inmate, surprisingly, told us that he made his way out to I-40 and drove that marked car from here to Castle Hayne. I found that hard to believe.

Our staff was down there near this gentleman's house, and here the inmate comes walking down the street wearing the deputy's coat, carrying that 9-millimeter. We're in a very close residential neighborhood, so my staff wisely made the decision not to shoot. I happened to be up here when the call came in that he had been spotted. Needless to say, we made it down there posthaste.

We set up a perimeter. The inmate went to the door. We had already been there and talked to the gentleman. The inmate's girlfriend and her two kids were in this house. He went to the front door, knocked and they would not let him in. So the inmate went around into the garage and apparently entered the house through a side door that entered the house from the garage. They retreated to the bedroom and locked themselves in the bedroom.

Well, he made them open the door and got in there and said, "Man, you got to help me." They said they couldn't do it. He looks over and sees the guy's car keys on the dresser, grabs them, runs out the front door, jumps in and takes off. He comes to a cul-de-sac with nowhere to go, so he takes off across backyards in this truck. He hits a privacy fence behind one of those houses and disables the truck, jumps out of the truck, still carrying that 9-millimeter, and runs into a wooded area next to this house.

We still got the perimeter maintained, so he's not going anywhere. He's in those woods somewhere. We were setting up spotlights around him, kind of like in the movies, but I had an uneasy feeling—I really had an uneasy feeling—that somebody was going to get hurt. In my career I have probably worked 130 to 140 escapes, and this was one of those handful that I had an uneasy feeling about. The man's still armed, he's running, he's desperate, it's night and he's in a wooded area. So we made the decision we would enter that area with members of our PERT team and a K-9 unit, and we found him hiding in a ditch. He had discarded the pistol and gave up. It did have a happy ending after all, but it had given me an uneasy feeling.

The Barber of Burgaw: Ray Rivenbark

I don't diagnose it, but I tell them what I know about it.

The eighty-year-old man who had come for a haircut had also come for courage. Tall, lean and wearing a flannel shirt and gray trousers, he sat in Ray Rivenbark's barber chair and spoke anxiously of a family member's upcoming wedding: his desire to show up presentable, to be noticed and to be well liked.

"Razor" Ray, owner of Ideal Barber Shop in Burgaw for the past forty years, looked down over him, gently wet his hair and, complimenting his customer's youth, switched on hair clippers, enveloping the room in a pleasant buzz. Amid clippers droning and hair falling, the man talked in spurts about getting to the wedding and what to say to the bride and groom.

In the background, Ray's black boombox belted "There'll Be Peace in the Valley" against powder-blue walls and blue-green bottles of Barbicide. The black narrow combs within stood at attention like the groomsmen I imagined at the wedding. On a wall a diploma read "Durham Institute of Barbering, 1962."

As Ray's reassurances grew more and more, the man began to laugh, even joke, until he bounced up out of the chair, passed Ray a sawbuck and scooted across the black-and-white-checkered floor out the door.

Ray smiled, crossed his muscular arms, sat down in the chair and spoke about changes in hairstyles, his community and how he came to barber in Burgaw.

An old barber, a fellow I worked under, once told me: "Ten years from now you won't have the same business—you'll have more business or less business, but you won't have the same business." In my experience as a barber I have found that story to be very true. People have moved away. They have died. They have wanted change. Some people's hair I've cut from the time they were born until they had grandchildren. Some families I've cut five generations.

The barbering school is just to learn the basics of a haircut, and you also have to study a book. When I went to school, 85 was passing. Anything below 85 as far as your book work was a failing grade. You learned such things as the nervous system, anatomy, the circulatory system and the skeletal system, things of that nature. My wife was in nurses' training, and we talked a lot about anatomy.

The history of barbering goes way back. The barber is mentioned in the book of Leviticus. You had to learn the names of the muscles and stuff like that. If somebody came in with a disease or something or another, you'd recognize it and say, "Hey, you need to go to the doctor." Sometimes the doctor doesn't bother to tell them what it is, but I have a textbook and I can open it up and say, "This is what you have." I don't diagnose it, but I tell them what I know about it.

They teach you how to shave first. There are about seven steps or different positions you hold your razor in to shave someone. We started out by putting tape over the blade for the first few times, and the instructors would come around and say, "Hey, you need to hold the blade this way or that way." We'd shave one another. After the first day you'd take that tape off. We had to shave every day. About the second day we started cutting hair. They had an instructor that would always clean the haircut up—for the most part you'd leave with a pretty good haircut.

I took a hairstyling course and, of course, when you cut hair you style it to a person's desire. That's what hairstyling is about, cutting it to a person's personal likes. Through the years it's changed from one style to another, from full with no sideburns to long and full over the ears like a lady's cut back to real short like a buzz haircut, and now it's beginning to turn back into a longer cut.

Talk about mohawks, I've cut two mohawks, and for the most part both of them I cut have been through bets. A young group of boys will get together, and one will say, "If you get one, I'll get one too." I had a little six-year-old come in with his uncle, and he got one. His momma was surprised big time. Of course, when it grew out enough to get it back to the right length, his momma brought him in for the next haircut.

A Revolutionary Place: Gary E. Trawick

And all of a sudden you realize that we're all just folks...

Sitting down in Judge Gary Trawick's second-story garage office within walking distance of the courthouse, I sensed we were not alone.

Something seemed to be looking down on us with impartiality. Perhaps this force permeated the large square room that boasted mint-green walls; a bright yellow, blue and purple Native American–themed rug; and books with titles like *The Science of the Mind* and *The Trial of Jesus*.

Ahead of me, on a wood desk so massive you could see the heads of the bolts that kept it forced together, was mounted the seal of the state of North Carolina, almost the size of a wagon wheel. In spaces beside and above the seal resided a charcoal rendering of the bow-tied and bespectacled Judge Trawick reading, a trophy with a football player stiff-arming the air, a mallard duck and a fly rod.

As Judge Trawick, a state special superior court judge for the past eleven years, and I spoke about the colonial history of Pender County and his memories growing up and practicing law in Burgaw, there remained the feeling of being watched.

At this point I turned to see Lady Justice—all seven feet of her— behind me in a corner blindfolded with her left arm raised holding a lantern. What looked like a Hollywood prop suddenly brought the room in closer, reinforcing the careful balance of the laws—past and present, man-made and natural—that maintain Pender County.

I was raised in Burgaw. My folks came here when I was about a year old. My daddy came up from the panhandle part of Florida to work in the shipyard during the war. So I've lived here for more than sixty years. I went to high school here, went off to Carolina Law School, came home and practiced law here for twenty-six years and I've been a Superior Court judge for eleven years, traveling all over the state.

I had a general law practice that did everything. When I started practicing law, I went in with an older man who hadn't practiced in several years because he had throat cancer. He had a bunch of books and I had a bunch of energy. So we took off. I got an extra room from First Citizens Bank. They charged me $15 a month. I didn't have enough money to put my name on the door, so I went down to Pope's (which was kind of a five-and-dime store) and bought some stencils and stenciled my name on the door with paint. Harold Pollock, later my law partner, got the bank to let him have the window. So now I've got the window that I painted my name on when I started practicing law. I bought a used desk from a fellow named Cavanaugh at a used furniture place, and I think the desk cost me $20, and I bought a chair for $12 and I was in the law business.

There was an old oil heater over at the bank, and in the winter I'd have to go down and get oil out of a drum and take it up and put it in the heater and light the heater. Then I'd go to Durham's drugstore and drink coffee till it got warm enough up there, and then the problem was that it would overheat. Then you'd have to go raise the windows and let the heat out. The train still ran then. The train would run and vibrate the building and dust would come down. And your desk would be covered with dust that would come down from the plaster. That's how I started.

Back then we had a typewriter and you used carbon paper. We finally got a copy machine that you put one of those pink sheets on, heat it some way and of course after five or six years the copy would fade and go out. Other than the secretary's salary and a little telephone bill, that was the only overhead you had. When I quit practicing law, my telephone bill was more money than I made the first year I practiced law. That's how things have changed. Of course, nobody had a computer. I got the first automatic typewriter in town. It had a display. It had a one-line display, so the secretary could type a line and correct that one line and, man, I thought I was in tall cotton.

I represented kids who got their first traffic tickets, and then I represented them when they got married and when they were buying their first house. I drew their wills. I settled their parents' estate. If they got in an automobile wreck, I'd represent them in that. And finally they had children, and you represented some of their children when they got their traffic tickets. You developed a bond that was not based on business—they'd just call you up. I've had widows come by and ask me, you know, they were trading automobiles and wanted to know if I thought it was a good deal and if they should go ahead and trade. And I felt that obligation back to them. And you knew everybody, and you kind of had a standard fee for services, but you adjusted it based on what you knew people's abilities to pay were. And you felt like—because you were a lawyer—you had an obligation to help anybody that needed help regardless of whether they could pay or not.

For the first couple hundred years or so Pender was tied to New Hanover County. There are things like the Battle of Moore's Creek, one of those things that happened here in this county that I think is understated in American history books. You talk about Lexington-Concord, those types of events, but had the Highlanders united with the British, the Revolution could have come out entirely different. So there are some things that happened here like that that I don't think we really appreciate to the extent we ought to.

We don't talk anymore about Timothy Bloodworth. Timothy Bloodworth was from this county, and he was one of the first congressmen under the Articles of Confederation and was a friend of Thomas Jefferson's. He led this state not to ratify the U.S. Constitution and resigned from Congress to campaign against the Constitution. And he is probably one of the people most responsible for the addition of the Bill of Rights because he feared a strong federal, central government. He influenced the path that this nation went on. He was somebody who had very significant impact well beyond this county.

The Rocky Point area of Pender County at the time just prior to the Revolution, in my opinion, had the absolute strongest political influence of any geographical area in the colony. You had Moseley, who had been acting governor; you had the Lillingtons; you had Samuel Swan, Speaker of the Assembly; and you got all the Ashes. Then there's Maurice Moore, a brother of Roger Moore of Orton Plantation. The Moores are the ones responsible for the settlement of Pender County.

The Tuscarora Indians up in New Bern killed John Lawson. They stuck lightwood splinters in him and burned him to death. He was a surveyor. Of course, the Indians seemed to realize that when he started surveying, somebody came and took the land. So North

A Revolutionary Place: Gary E. Trawick

Carolina called on South Carolina for some help. The proprietors did not really want to settle southeastern North Carolina. They were kind of holding it out—they wanted to turn southeastern North Carolina into a New England–type of settlement with small villages with small farms outside of it. Of course, being over in England they didn't really understand the lay of the land. Down here you can't lay out forty acres and not have a whole bunch of swampland. The land is not uniform like it is up in the New England states. Well, the Moores came from the Goose Creek section down near Charleston. And they went up to fight the Indians.

The Indians were pretty tough. They had done stuff like cut the bellies of pregnant women open and thrown the fetuses up in trees. Moore has an entry in some of his correspondence that when he and his men came up here and defeated the Indians that they engaged in "exquisite torture."

You see the Indians believed in a supreme creator god, and they believed that you were going to go to the happy hunting ground. And they believed everybody got there—they even had a kind of purgatory concept that if you had been bad you would go through stages, and eventually, though, you were going to get to the happy hunting ground. And so based on that belief, if you just killed somebody you really were helping them out because you were sending them to the happy hunting ground. And so the only way to really punish them was to torture them, so the Indians engaged in torture.

Janet Shaw, the woman who wrote diaries before the Revolution, described Moore as someone who was pretty capable of doing just about anything. He had all the genteel manners, but she saw a hardness in him. He was bragging that he and his men had engaged in the "exquisite torture" of these Indians. They not only drove the Indians out, they also passed through…and they realized there was a big hunk of land here—good land.

And so they had political connections to come up and start getting land grants. Pender County was settled by people seeking cheap land. Proprietors started inserting rules to keep people from having these great big grants. What they would do is they'd say you could only have a grant for so many people. But folks like the Moores brought all their black Americans with them, who of course were slaves at the time, and they would apply for however many acres it was for each one of them. And they still got huge grants,

In modern times and especially during the colonial era, timber and related byproducts made the Pender and Lower Cape Fear regions prosper. *Courtesy of the Pender County Library.*

Picnic at Moore's Creek Revolutionary War Battleground, site of a decisive Patriot victory against Scottish Highlanders in the early morning hours of February 27, 1776. *Courtesy of the Pender County Museum.*

and they came and established their homes and so forth along the river because the river was a primary artery for transportation back and forth to Wilmington.

There's a story about the Moores meeting with Governor Burrington down at Rocky Point, and he was down there to stake his claim. They told the governor, "Huh, eh, we were here first buddy. This is our land." So Burrington came up and staked out Stag Park. He came farther up the river. I talked to some people just a year ago who've lived a long time down at Stag Park. And the woman told me that her husband wasn't home, but she thought he was "on the park." They still use that terminology: "on the park." I thought that was kind of unusual.

The western part of the county didn't develop as quickly because the lower portions of the Black River all have swamp for some considerable period away from the river. And so the western part of the county actually developed much farther up toward the Ivanhoe and Sampson County area.

I remember when [Hurricane] Hazel came through here when I was a little boy in 1954. I was nine years old. We lived over on the other side of the town; we lived over on what essentially we referred to as the "park." It was one of those typical towns where the railroad track kind of divided the black section and the white section. For the first twelve years I lived over on the fringes of the black section. A lot of my playmates were black. That's where I was when Hazel came through. And I can remember it coming—we had a great big pear tree and, of course, it blew all the pears off. And when the eye came through we went out and picked the pears up. We thought the storm was about over. Then the backside came and we had to go back in the house.

Hazel took a toll on this county. It really took a toll on the beaches. It was years before the beach got back. Around here it [destroyed] mostly trees and tobacco barns. Of course, tobacco was big back then and you had the traditional kinds of tobacco barns. One of the big things when I worked in tobacco growing up was for us to ride around at night checking the barns because the heat had to be regulated. And that gave you a legitimate excuse to be out riding around. So of course you could get into a whole lot of other stuff, but all you had to do was go down and look at the thermometer and cut it up or down. You would tell your parents you were out "checking barns."

Schools, of course, were different. You called it Burgaw High School, but basically there was one building that had the first three grades and that was like the grammar school. Then in the main building you had grades four through eight, which was kind of like middle school. So high school was actually exactly what it says: you went to the second floor. You moved over to the main building. You thought that you'd died. And then when you got to the ninth grade through the twelfth grade, you actually got to the second floor, and all those classes were upstairs so you were actually in "high" school.

Obviously, there was racial division; there still is racial division. I realize how much it cost me when I realize that Samm-Art Williams—who won a Tony nomination, was one of the writers for [*The*] *Fresh Prince* [*of Bel-Air*], one of the producers on *Frank's Place* on TV, and he and I are about the same age—that I never met Samm-Art until he came to me to do some legal work after I was back here practicing law. And so here we were raised in the same town, and I always had so much respect for him because Samm-Art, despite the fact that blacks were discriminated against—there's no question about it—it didn't scar him. He still lives in Burgaw. He told me this is where real people were. I realize if I had known Samm-Art, my life would have been richer.

But I lived over in that part, and we'd play basketball together, and then when you worked in tobacco, we just worked together. And all of a sudden you realize that we're all just folks, and they got hot and sweaty just like you.

When I was growing up and dove season came it was a big deal, as all hunting was. Today, to go dove hunting you almost have to be invited somewhere. Back then if you went down to Futch's Esso at eleven in the morning—see, you couldn't start shooting till twelve o'clock—somebody had organized a dove hunt. And everybody who wanted to go could just go. So you just met down there, and it wasn't one of these deals you had to be especially invited kind of thing. Again, you were just included. You didn't have to know somebody or be somebody. And the older men wanted the boys to go. It wasn't like you were extra baggage. And they were not your daddy. My daddy didn't hunt. But they would take you out, and if you were not hitting doves or something, they would make suggestions to you and so forth.

It was a social occasion, and it was also a time when boys got to be with men, and everybody was having a good time, and you were treated on an equal basis with the adults. And I think it has a lot to do with the way that we grew up interacting with people. We did the same kind of thing going to shad fries and herring fries. You see, herring used to come up the river, and we would catch herring way on up the river. You caught them in a net. The herring came up a little ahead of the shad. But the herring doesn't come up the river anymore. We would have big cookouts, and again the boys would get to come down just like the men did. And you would help cook and help do things, and it introduced you to an adult life. You saw it and you experienced it.

Weathering the Storm:
Virginia Stokes Rochelle

I was a pioneer.

Virginia Stokes Rochelle remembers days when, as a teacher in Pender County, she stood at the chalkboard for hours without sitting. She also remembers the pay: $289 a month. Most of all, she remembers—sometimes painfully—the stone throwing and name calling she experienced as one of the county's first black teachers in a desegregated classroom.

Dressed in a stylish purple pantsuit and beige blouse, the now-retired teacher and former Burgaw town commissioner introduced herself with perfect elocution and a firm handshake, prompting me like a young schoolchild to straighten my posture.

According to Mrs. Rochelle, Pender County began desegregating its public schools in the late 1960s. During this transition, she was assigned in 1967 to Penderlea High School, a few miles north of Burgaw. Two other high school students composed the entire black student body that first year.

How she described the two students' plights—their separation even during lunch period, how daily they lugged the weight of ugly stares and words—brought new meaning to an old conflict. She remained the master teacher throughout the telling, careful not to let her emotions overwhelm the purpose of her lesson.

As she exited the library and walked down the sidewalk with her head up and shoulders square, a giant shimmering wave of spring air and nearby lilacs seemed to push ahead of her, undoing all obstacles. In seconds she turned a corner and was gone.

I came here to teach school in 1959. I was twenty years old. Didn't know anything. There was one traffic light. First Citizens Bank was where the Laney Real Estate office is now. And I'm trying to think if First National had yet come at that time. There were a lot of shops at that time. You could do some nice shopping in Burgaw. I remember Mrs. Lucas had a shop, and she catered to the teachers because we were the ones, she said, that had the money.

I was bringing home $289 a month, and that was a lot of money. We were well dressed. We wore our heels and stockings, and we wore our dresses or our suits or blouses and skirts. We did not wear pants. And we had a command in the classroom because of our position, the way we dressed, the way we carried ourselves. We knew how to stand at the chalkboard and move our feet in the right direction as you moved down the chalkboard. We didn't sit on the tops of desks. We sat in a chair when we needed to sit. But I never learned to sit. I taught thirty-three years, and I never really learned to sit to teach. I was a moving teacher because I wanted to be hands-on with the kids.

Being an elementary school major, I taught it all until we began to specialize and get into departmentalization. I taught everything, and when I got fifteen years into my career, I was a reading specialist. That meant I was able to teach all of the elementary, and then I taught four years in the high school for reading. So I got a chance to teach all the grades before I retired.

I was a part of desegregation. I was the first black teacher to teach at Penderlea. It was a high school because it had grades one through twelve at that particular time, the same as Burgaw High School. Everybody was on the same campus. I was a pioneer. When I first came here, I came here to teach. That was my ultimate reason to come. My aim was to stay one year, get experience and move on. As we rode that Sunday afternoon coming here, I kept saying to the person who had worked here previously, "Are you sure this is in North Carolina?"

So I get to Burgaw, a small town. I room with a family because there are no places for single teachers to live, no apartments as we have all these apartments today. So there were several families that were on a list, and when the principal hired you, he would send you a list of those families, and you would have to contact the family to see if they would receive you as one of the persons in their home to live. So the first family I wrote to was Mrs. Georgiana Clarke: she always took in teachers. So she wrote me a nice letter back and said that her house would not be suitable for me because she had seven boys. She had no girls. She directed me to one of her church members, so I wrote Mrs. Montague and lived with her. I had a room, and she did my cooking, fixed my lunch and did my laundry all for $50 a month. Remember now, I didn't make but $289 a month.

I found coming here from a big city to a small town very embracing. The people embraced me. I fell in love with Burgaw, and I think Burgaw fell in love with me. When I came here and accepted my job, we were told we would have to visit the homes of all of our students, and we would need to attend church services. Well, this was a way you got to know the people. And going into the home gave you an opportunity to know more about what you needed to do to teach that child because you would see the environment that the child was in. I think today if teachers were mandated to make home visitations it might be a different day. Now grant you, we didn't always get inside those homes. Sometimes they would meet you in the yard, but you still had an opportunity to make contact. And I wore out a lot of tires trying to find out why children were not coming to school because we had to go and find out why a student was out so many days. Why was this child absent? And sometimes they were out because they had to work. Or they were picking cotton, too.

And we didn't always have the best books, now. Mostly we had the secondhand books. Very rarely did we have a new book. From '59 up until '64, we were still getting secondhand books. Very few new books came in, and we didn't have a cafeteria at the beginning. We had what you called a canteen where you could get milk—remember the old Quonset huts they would use on the army bases?—that's what they used for the cafeteria building. Because, remember, we were grades one through twelve because it was C.F. Pope High School, but all the grades were housed in that facility. I think it might have been toward the end of '60 or first part of '61 that we got a cafeteria.

In the classroom, I worked in what they called the Old Gray Building where we had wooden floors, and they would use the oil on the floors to try to keep the dust down. We had the potbelly stove, and a child was assigned to go to the coal pile each day to bring in coal. The janitor would start the fire for you, but you had to keep the fire going. And nobody was going to come and stoke the fire for you. We always fixed a chart showing who would be responsible for going to the coal pile. The janitor would come and sweep the floors in the afternoon, but in between if you needed anything, you had to do it yourself.

We had anywhere from thirty to thirty-five kids in a classroom. You didn't have these small-size classes, and you didn't have the aide or the assistant or the paraprofessional to help you. You were

Virginia Stokes Rochelle, educator and former Burgaw town commissioner. *Courtesy of Mrs. Virginia Stokes Rochelle.*

C.F. POPE SCHOOL
Formerly Burgaw Normal and Industrial School

The Pender County Board of Education was ordered to desegregate by the fall of 1969. Here, students graduate in 1913 from the all-black C.F. Pope High School in Burgaw. *Courtesy of the Pender County Library.*

it all day long. And we didn't have the copy machines that you have now. We had what was a jelly substance that you would put into a mold and you would write out your lessons and then you'd put it on there and make a print. And then you'd copy from that. Sometimes you'd run several copies before you'd have to redo the surface again. This was how we did our duplicating.

My involvement at Penderlea High School did not come until 1966–67. We didn't become desegregated I think until 1966–67, and that was when they were doing it voluntarily. The strange thing was there were only two black kids at Penderlea, and they were in high school, and I felt so sorry for those kids because they were not in the same grade. They were at the end of the line and nobody wanted them there. And I thought it was so cruel that the parents had sent them there because they had to fight that thing every day. They didn't even have lunch together. I will never forget them. I did not have a good life at Penderlea High School as far as some of the students and parents were concerned because, remember, they didn't want me either.

The faculty was fine. The principal, Mr. Carl Weaver, I'll always love because he was really good. It was a new day for them. I had no choice. When I was assigned to Penderlea I couldn't say, "I don't want to go there." So there were three black people there: two students and myself. I had no contact with them because they were in high school. I taught seventh and eighth grade. I had social studies—that's what I taught. Before we desegregated some of the schools did not allow blacks to teach math and English. We only taught what they called the "it doesn't matter" subjects. This is the way it was. We're talking thirty-nine years ago. So I went in, I did a fantastic job as best I could: I had to dodge rocks, beans and corn kernels. I had to stand with my back to the corner. I could never turn my back to the students. They eventually hired Mrs. Ruth Carr to come in and sit with me—just to sit in that room, so I could teach. That's what I had to go through. But that was the time. And it made me a better person. It made me more understanding. It gave me an opportunity to move from Penderlea to Burgaw High because of the way I had conducted myself. I had beautiful lesson plans. I tried to execute them. I did the very best I could under the circumstances.

One night we had a PTA meeting at Penderlea. Dudley Robbins was the chairman of the board of education, and I had said to him, "I don't feel good about coming out here to the PTA meeting because I've had so much difficulty during the daylight hours." I said, "The night has a thousand eyes, the day has but one." He said, "Well, I'll have the Pender County Sheriff's Department out here to be sure nothing happens." There was no sheriff when we arrived. I had bought a brand new '66 Mercury. I did not drive that out there that night because they had already marked that up with pencils and things.

My husband was with me, and we drove our truck, so he stayed in the truck. We had not gotten any more than fifteen minutes into that meeting when my husband came to the door and said, "My wife's going to have to come out here, and we're going to have to leave." They, whoever, were out there rocking that truck back and forth. Remember, they didn't want me there, and it wasn't my fault that I was there. I didn't ask to go. This was my assignment. So I came out of the meeting, and my husband and I left. The principal and the faculty I will always love: they decided I would never have to come out there for anything else. "Whatever has to be done, and you have to do it at night," they said, "we will do it for you." It was very threatening to everybody to go back for anything at night.

There were parents who would tell their children in the evening, "You go to school every day, and you be just as mean and just as nasty as you can be." So if they didn't want to do it, they were fed. Really and truly when you look at little children, they don't know hate. It's a learned behavior.

Weathering the storm at Penderlea helped me to get ready for the job in town. Richard Uzzell was principal at Burgaw High. He came to my house, and he said, "I know how you were treated at Penderlea, and I know that you are a good teacher. I've seen your lesson plans and I know you did the best you could. I want you to come to my school." So I did in 1967. That made me feel good that he came to my house to give me a job because I had passed the test.

When I came to Burgaw High School, this is where you had doctors' children—the Peedins, the Dees, and there were the Johnsons. You see, these were all families of my first class. No problem, except one. And I never will forget this boy. He and his daddy came in there, and they saw there was a black teacher, and his daddy snatched him up: "You ain't going to stay in here with this nigger," he said. So he took him out and went into town and began to talk to people at Dees' Drugstore—getting a listening ear, you know—so Mary Peedin was in there, and she said, "Let me tell you something. She is a fine teacher. Our Jimmy is in there. So-and-so is in there. And you better get yourself together!"

And after they told him that their boys were in there, and that what I had wasn't going to rub off on him—that when he goes back home he's still going to be white, he won't be black—the boy's daddy brought him back. He told his son, "You go over there and sit, and you do whatever she tells you to do." The boy's daddy thought he would poison other people against me, but they already knew who I was, and they knew what I had gone through at Penderlea, and they knew that I could teach. And I did.

The Unorthodox Orthodox:
Annette Boryk Oppegaard

In fact, I still have the chest that my grandparents brought with all their possessions.

Never would I have thought that plowshares from Pender County had so much in common with brick archways from New York's Ellis Island, until I spoke with Topsail Island resident and St. Helena native Annette Boryk Oppegaard.

The granddaughter of a Ukrainian family that settled just south of Burgaw at the turn of the century, Annette grew up farming lettuce and cabbage alongside her Catholic mother and Russian Orthodox father.

Believing the South's long-standing problems with sharecropping and tenant farming could be remedied by offering European immigrants the chance to till American soil, well-known Wilmington land developer Hugh MacRae attracted hundreds of immigrants with the promise of a three-room cottage and a ten-acre farm for $240. The first families arrived from Italy between 1905 and 1907. Others from Poland, Holland, Germany, Hungary and Ukraine, including the Boryk family, followed.

When I asked about language barriers, Mrs. Oppegaard drew a big smile and let go a sentence filled with the sounds ch, sh and zh. She explained that around the house with her grandmother she spoke only Ukrainian, while her formal introduction to the English language came when she attended public school.

Her family's labor in St. Helena's fields, their modest living and their gradual acquisition of land on nearby Topsail Island (now one of the region's top beach destinations) underscores the immigrant experience and desires for identity, prosperity and belonging.

Michael Andrew Boryk, father of Annette Boryk Oppegaard. St. Helena, North Carolina. *Courtesy of Mrs. Annette Boryk Oppegaard.*

My father bought a cottage in Topsail Beach in 1956. We spent our summers and weekends there, but before that my father and my uncle, Jim Pecora, built a cottage over on Lee Island, which we had to come to by boat. And you would come to Hampstead and go by boat over to Lee Island. Before that time, my grandfather, who was John Gmytruk from Castle Hayne, had a fishing camp over there and that's how we were introduced to the coast of Pender County.

When my father bought property at Topsail and we had the cottage there, he started buying more property. And he was quite a horse trader too. At one time my father owned the assembly building, which is now where the Missiles and More Museum is. He traded that piece of property for the motel site where Sea Vista Motel is, and then he did a tax exchange for the Sea Vista Motel. From where our business was on Florida Avenue South is what Slim Anderson and my daddy developed, and then they took in a partner, Bernard McCloud.

And my grandfather built his camp back in the 1940s, and it was strictly a fishing camp because you had lanterns for electricity, and

The 1933 wedding of Michael Andrew Boryk and Anna Gmytruk Boryk, parents of Annette Boryk Oppegaard. *Courtesy of Mrs. Annette Boryk Oppegaard.*

OWN A HOME
—IN—
NORTH CAROLINA

This is the 3-room cottage which we offer to build for our settlers for $240,----$90 cash, balance in three equal yearly payments.
Carolina Trucking Development Co.
WILMINGTON, N. C.

FORM 503

Original handbill advertising Hugh MacRae's St. Helena colony. *Courtesy of the Pender County Library.*

The Unorthodox Orthodox: Annette Boryk Oppegaard

St. Helena colonists await the arrival of new immigrants. They often brought their instruments to celebrate. *Courtesy of the Pender County Library.*

it still doesn't have electricity. It's a little island south of Topsail Beach, and we would go on weekends. My parents farmed. My father was a contractor. He had his contractor's license. Going back to my grandparents, my father's parents came over from the Ukraine, and my uncle, John Boryk, was born in Europe. But my father was born here in the United States—in fact, in Ohio. Then my grandparents learned of the ten acres of land that Hugh MacRae was giving to immigrants if they would come and farm. My grandparents came to Pender County. A lot of the immigrants, as they were coming into Ellis Island, were aware of other families already in Pender County at St. Helena. In fact, I still have the chest that my grandparents brought with all their possessions. That was it. They were very dedicated. When they moved to Pender County, they farmed. And he would haul the produce and sell it when he first started.

St. Helena had a central place where they baked bread. During the war there was also a cannery in Burgaw where they canned food. My father would drive his vegetable truck during World War II, and he would sell vegetables and trade some things and bring things back for Mother—things that you just couldn't get.

Sts. Peter and Paul Russian Orthodox Church. Built in 1932 by St. Helena residents, it was the first of its kind in North Carolina. *Courtesy of Mrs. Anne Debaylo Mizerak.*

At this particular time nylon hose was a luxury. Both my parents had fourth-grade educations. Both of them worked in the fields…Now, Mother lost a child at birth, her name was Mary Anne, and then a year later my brother was born and that was in 1939. He graduated from Burgaw, went to North Carolina State University to major in horticulture, and he was in his last semester at NC State and came home and told Dad, "I'm going to farm with you." And so he did not go back. But he came back and farmed and married a girl from Smithfield who was at East Carolina University, and they did not have any children.

She [my sister-in-law] taught at Burgaw High School. My brother was killed in an accident. I think they had been married about four years. That was when I was in my second year of teaching at the parochial school in Richmond, and so we had five hundred acres of fruits and vegetables, so I came home. As a child, my grandmother and I were in charge of the house and the meals, the laundry and everything else. After dinner, everybody would come and eat, and I would go up to the produce market, and I was in charge of doing all the manifests and answering the telephone. This was eight, nine, ten years old that I started to do this. I grew up into it. This was all manual labor and we hired folks from the community.

My mother bought an old school bus the county had gotten rid of, and she would start at six o'clock in the morning and go pick up all the help, and she would make sure during school time that my brother and I were up, and my grandmother would fix breakfast for us. Grandmother would fix breakfast for us, and we would go off to school. We started farming in January—we would make our lettuce beds just like they do the tobacco beds. You use cheesecloth and make your mounds. You mound up your dirt on the side, and then in the bed you sew your seed, and then you had cheesecloth on top. When it was cold weather, you would cover up your plants, so they wouldn't freeze.

So we started in January with our lettuce beds and our cabbage beds, and then my father built hothouses. We grew the first cauliflower in North Carolina. We grew the first broccoli in North Carolina. This was seed bought from New Jersey. As we progressed, and he bought trucks, and we started selling things, he would send to Richmond, Philadelphia, New York and Boston. Those were his shipping places. They packed the produce with ice, and they had a motor that would keep it cool. My father every morning would start at 5:30, calling the different brokers, asking, "What do you need today? What do you need by the end of the week?"

My father had never gone to Florida. Slim Anderson, whose father developed Topsail Beach, went down to Immokalee. Slim Anderson (J.G. Anderson Jr.) farmed down there. Slim talked my father into coming down to Immokalee to do some shipping of vegetables. And so they went down one year, and they were doing fruits and vegetables, and my father couldn't get help up at the packing shed where they were packing the vegetables. So my mother told Slim, "Let me have the truck. I'll get you some help." She went into an unknown community and recruited. She had no fear. And she got people to come and help. She just had that special whatever it takes. She was a hard worker. She was the one that maintained the people in the fields. My father was the one that did the packaging and the shipping. My brother was the one that kept the tractors up and ordered the fertilizer and got all the details of the mechanical parts going, and my job was with my grandmother in the house and then in the evening up at the pack shed.

My mother was Roman Catholic. My father was Russian Orthodox. She was from the community of Castle Hayne, which is in New Hanover County. And it was always a little bit of a struggle which church we were going to go to: to the Orthodox church or to the Catholic church? My brother and I went to a Catholic school in St. Helena—and I'm not sure if it was the Mercy Nuns—but the nuns lived in the convent. They moved the church from St. Helena to Castle Hayne, and when they did that Mother put us in public school, and it was at that time that my parents sat down as a family, and my father said, "Let's all join one church together." He gave up the Orthodox church, she gave up the Roman Catholic church and we went to St. Mary's Episcopal. We didn't have a Sunday school—there weren't many children— so I would go to Sunday school at the Presbyterian church and then come to church at the Episcopal church. It was my brother and myself and maybe two or three more young people. We were very diverse.

Let me tell you about Mr. Rowe's theater. Growing up as children in the little town of Burgaw on Saturday morning, we'd tidy up the house and on Saturday afternoon my mother would go and have her hair done, and when she had her hair done and did the grocery shopping, she would take us to the movie theater and leave us. We all went to the movies together and just had fun. It was just like kids go to the mall now. It was a sharing time. Mr. Worsley—from one of the Worsleys in Warsaw—he was one that collected the tickets, and they had a little stand for popcorn drinks and candy. And then you would go in through double doors, and it was slanted down so everybody could see the movie. That was our Saturday afternoon activity. The town was very relaxed.

Hampstead Spot:
Edwin and Julia Moseley Combs

What people hold on to is very important.

It seemed the future finally caught up with the past the morning I drove to Ed and Julia Combs's home at Olde Point Golf and Country Club in Hampstead along U.S. 17 in the eastern part of the county. On a gracious lot with a one-story ranch house and tall pine trees, a man wearing a hunter orange cap on a tractor dragged behind him a long steel pipe—what I later learned to be a drill. I had arrived just in time to see workers begin tunneling through the neighborhood to make way for municipal water and sewer: a first for the Combs family and their neighbors.

It was far different when the Combses first arrived as retirees in 1974, having returned to their native North Carolina after living twenty-seven years just outside Washington, D.C. The land was wild with azaleas and mosquitoes, they said, an out-of-the-way purchase that baffled friends and relatives.

Once described as "a wide spot in the middle of the road" with a history that included a visit by George Washington in 1791, over the past decade Hampstead has become one of the flagship communities of the Pender County coastline.

In their living room, a quiet place with a picture window (where tractors now passed back and forth in front like red ants), Ed and Julia handed me a collection of sun-faded folders, the top one titled "The Greater Hampstead Civic Association." Inside, minutes from meetings dating back to 1978 discussed everything from dumpsters and traffic lights to book drives and redistricting.

As I ran my fingers across pages that were surely clues to Hampstead's present-day design, a feeling of cool shade and ocean breezes overtook me. It was not for long, however, as men in helmets kicked through brush and cranked up their tractors.

Julia: We retired in 1974 and returned to North Carolina. We were roughly the twelfth house at Olde Point. There was nothing across the street. Even the road you came in on was not in place. We had to go down Country Club Road to King's Landing and come back up to get in here. Then they opened up King's Landing Road, put the little bridge across the creek, you know. It was rural, really country. I think there was one little store—well, it's called a grocery store—but it was just odds and ends, very small, and you could count on getting bread or milk or little things like that, but we had to go all the way into Wilmington to get groceries.

It was a long drive to Wilmington back then, of course. There wasn't much between here and there, but you can see how much traffic there is now. Coming into Hampstead from Wilmington we had those big oak trees with Spanish moss on them. It was so pretty, but they're all going so fast.

When we bought property in here, we didn't know the plans for Olde Point. At the time we moved, Mr. Harvey Jones, who owned the property, was just developing Topsail Greens golf course. And he had an original Queen Anne land grant, which gave him property on both sides of the sound—all the way across the water to the beach. And he was developing that golf course. I think at the time, couldn't you just go out there and play on what he had?

Edwin: Until he finished the eighteen, you could go out there and play all he had.

Julia: At that time there was Buddy Mizzell, who operated a head boat off Topsail Island, and in the wintertime he liked to bring his boat across the sound to his home on the land side of the sound, and so Mr. Jones dug a channel across so that he could bring the boat over. His right to do that was questioned. So Mr. Jones showed his Queen Anne land grant…that gave him the right to the channel right to the bottom. I don't know where the land grant was kept, whether he just had it in his home or what.

Edwin: A lot of the people in the coastal areas, if you went to their homes, they would have the land grants framed. Like this guy Jones—he came from the Nixon family. He's related to the Nixons, and they were one of the earliest land grant people. He had land grants out over the waterfront all the way up to Porters Neck. In fact, this is called Nixon's Creek right here in back of us.

Julia: What people hold on to is very important. In the eastern part of North Carolina, families have been here for years and years and generation after generation, so people accumulate a lot of family history. When I lived in Kinston, it was a little town of ten thousand people and almost everybody was kin to somebody. Half the town was kin to the other half. There was a lot of family history, and that's why they held on to these deeds.

Edwin: I was in scouting for fifty years, and the first thing we did when we came here was that I started a class to train scoutmasters. I did that for seven years. In the meantime, we were in the Greater Hampstead Civic Association. I don't recall the exact date—maybe 1974 or 1975.

Julia: We noticed in today's paper the Greater Hampstead Civic Association is having a forum on the candidates for election. Well, that was one of the first things the original society did. It was an election year. I can't remember the date, but that was one of the big projects they had back then.

Edwin: It still is—to have public candidates.

Julia: It was just a little sleepy crossroads when we came, just a pleasant place to live. This part of the county apparently never seemed too important to the other side of the county. They always felt like stepchildren over here. They claimed they didn't get any attention. Of course, they didn't pay much in taxes because they just didn't have much to pay. We found everybody very friendly.

We knew that up in Burgaw, Ann Hoover Dees and Wayne Arnold were starting a class—I guess it was sponsored by the community college—but they were having a class on the history of genealogy. We thought we might get some information on genealogical resources, and that's how we got started in the Pender Historical Society. We didn't know much about the history of the county. I thought they had an unusual community interest—seems to me they worked together, and if there was

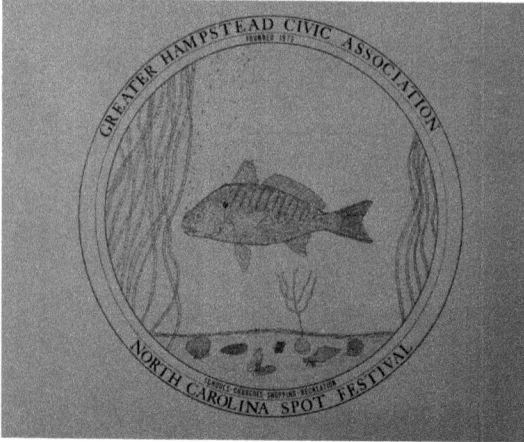

Ruth Hewitt's winning entry for the Greater Hampstead Civic Association's emblem contest, 1978. A confirmation letter reads: "The committee recommends that the Graphic Artist who puts this into final form ensures that the fish is indeed a spot…" *Courtesy of Mr. and Mrs. Edwin Combs.*

a project going on, they cooperated willingly. You didn't have to go around and beg for things. They always seemed to have a lot of community pride. We just found the people very interesting.

Edwin: One of the families here, the Lee family, was very prominent, and the youngest son, Hampton Lee, was in college with me. So when we moved here I spoke to Hamp again because we'd been at college at Wake Forest. And so they were a prominent family and he was sort of a celebrity. He ran the Spot Festival until he passed away. We met people that way; it was just a sleepy fishing town. There were two families that carried on the selling of fish—the Smith family and Lee family. Ordinary fishermen would go out there and catch fish and then sell them to the Lees or the Smiths. That had been the practice since it was a fishing town.

Julia: The Martha Ann Motel—I don't know if you noticed that or not when you came in at the intersection of Hoover Road and U.S. 17. One of the Lees, I believe it was Albert (he lived in Morehead), bought that, and when we came it had been sold to a Mrs. Herta Albrecht. I think she came down here from New York (I'm not sure) and she ran it and it is still a motel. We had a post office but it was very small. Now we're on our third post office—had to put up bigger buildings.

When we first came here, we had a little flatboat that we could ride around the shallow waters, and we bought equipment for

Hampstead Spot: Edwin and Julia Moseley Combs

House at Sloop Point Plantation. Dating back to 1726, the Hampstead house is believed to be the oldest in North Carolina. *Courtesy of the Pender County Library*.

shrimping—the big nets that you'd drop down—and we did quite a bit of shrimping right out in the creek. You could catch crabs, fish and oysters. We had so many good oysters. But over the years it's been overdone, overfished and I suppose all the home-building has contaminated it in ways because at one time they had to close the creek for shellfish. We still get crabs out there. You don't find many shrimp anymore. But when we first came, we had good shrimp. I remember writing a friend back in Maryland...and she said, "Don't tell anybody." But the secret got out without my telling it.

And when we built here, the house next door was already there, and they were building the one next to us—but beyond that there was nothing. There was nothing but woods. It was really what we had always looked for. We never had a big boat but we could go all through the sound. We just enjoyed poking around in all the little streams, estuaries and so forth.

Olde Point itself was just being developed. In fact, we had been all up and down the coast trying to find what we thought would be our dream house. And we just sort of stumbled on this. There was a rough sign out there on the highway that said something about Olde Point, and we just turned down out of curiosity—it was all muddy, you could hardly drive—but we knew right away it was what we wanted. The King family originally owned this land.

Edwin: Mr. Floyd Huffham came in to cut the timber off. He was a timber broker, and he bought the place…It runs about 350 acres. He cut the timber, and then he bought the plantation and decided to develop it.

Julia: After he bought this, he eventually bought the Sidbury Farm—another deep tract—and it's just grown.

Edwin: The Civic Association's first project here was when the people said they had to go all the way to Wilmington to use the library for the high school children to write their papers. So the first project we had was a book drive, and we got enough books so the children could do their papers right here in Hampstead. That worked into the library. The county didn't pay for it. The people in Hampstead got a grant from the state—two $50,000 grants to build the library—that was the next project we had. We built the library. After we built it, the county took it over, of course. Floyd Huffham gave the land where the library sits. Since then the library has expanded. They've already doubled the size of what it was originally. So that was the main push for the Civic Association. We had another guy who wanted to beautify, so he planted shrubs all up and down here.

The museum over on Topsail Island they've done extensive work on is about the missile-launching program the navy had in 1946. There was no bridge over to Surf City. The only bridge was a pontoon bridge.

Julia: The few families that were here when we first moved were so nice and friendly. Everybody would help everybody. I think the first year that we lived here that summer we had several trees blown down right in the creek. We woke up the next morning hearing chain saws. The neighbors had come in to help clean up.

The Clubhouse:
Johnny Westbrook

You had such great pleasure in doing the simplest things.

With one eye closed from just behind Johnny Westbrook's massive white drafting desk at the Burgaw Antiqueplace, I focused on a row of trees and signs a short distance beyond that pointed east to I-40 and Highway 53.

Like a surveyor looking through a scope, my limited perspective refreshed certain features of the Pender landscape I had come to take for granted: the pleasing effect of streets and rooftops at right angles, the gentle sway of pine tree bristles, sidewalks with vanishing points leading to areas overgrown with azalea and wisteria.

Hearing footsteps up an old wood staircase, I turned to see Johnny Westbrook, the building's owner and a Pender County native. Dressed in a red shirt and suspenders with a blue cap, the purveyor of antiques introduced himself, sat down and stroked his goatee.

Minutes into our conversation I realized that his life's work as the chief of the urban design divisions for the City of Baltimore, Maryland, and Montgomery County, North Carolina, uniquely qualified Johnny to speak about how things like memory and progress shape community.

Fittingly, against the backdrop of James Taylor's "Fire and Rain," Mr. Westbrook recalled the early days of the building we now occupied and how on a lot next door he and his friends used their imaginations to make simple pleasures everyday adventures.

> Everybody congregated in groups and this continued on through high school. These bonds were very strong, and the

mentor-worship you saw as a child would continue as you grew older. And you don't see kids playing basketball in the backyard anymore. They're inside watching TV and playing basketball with the latest basketball video game. So that bonding is not taking place on a community-wide basis.

There also seemed to be these clubs—it was little cliquey—but you'd have a clubhouse and we even took up dues. I remember my club, and you had a place where we hid the money. Now, what we did with the money I don't know, but it was sort of cool to collect dues. It was like if Momma and Daddy were ugly, we'd all band together and leave.

And then building treehouses—we had a three-story treehouse behind my house, and it had a roof over it. And it was something that you dream about: "What addition are we going to make next?" You had such great pleasure in doing the simplest things. For example, the building here [at Burgaw Antiqueplace] originally stopped about where you see the remnants of the wall. Daddy built that part in 1948, then came back in 1965 and bought this lot and added on and cantilevered over and grabbed the girders and then knocked the walls down. But up until that time this lot was vacant during my lifetime. Prior to that it had been a big Victorian house, but during my lifetime it was vacant and grew up with weeds. And Daddy would get these big boxes, and I would take the ends of them and fold them and then get inside of these boxes and walk with my hands like a bulldozer, making paths through the weeds in the lot right here. And the smell of this particular weed that was real fuzzy—occasionally it'll come up in the back, and I'll smell them and instantly I'm back and remember it.

Because these weeds would grow up—and they were real tall weeds—you could actually make forts out of them that would have roofs, so you would have these roofed little places that you could get in and play all kinds of games. And the games you played were real then—I mean you could be playing cowboys and Indians and stop at twelve o'clock and go back and start again exactly where you were in the storyline.

And Roy Rogers really was the king of cowboys and Hopalong Cassidy and gosh! there were just so many of them. So you would pretend you were one of these—Tonto and the Lone Ranger—and at Christmastime you would get the outfit. I did. I remember

North Wright Street in downtown Burgaw. The courthouse and the Confederate monument are to the right. *Courtesy of the Pender County Library.*

the Lash La Rue outfit I got one year. You've probably never heard of Lash La Rue. He had a whip and a black mask and black hat. But it was just so real. And the imagination that came from it was just a wonderful thing. Unfortunately I didn't like to read back then, but you created your own stories with your buddies.

And the freedom that you felt that I talked about before was real. It wasn't just something to be talked about; it was something that expanded your life. As an example: I guess I was about ten years old when I learned how to swim—there was no YMCA in Burgaw—and so Hugh Highsmith and I, who were best friends at the time (and he now owns Hugh Highsmith Fairway Ford), we would hop on the bus, ride it to Wilmington to the bus station and walk to Fourth and Market to the YMCA and take swimming lessons. Then, during the summertime the Y would have a softball team, so we'd play softball for a couple of hours, hop on the bus and come back.

Or other times I can remember riding to Moore's Creek Battleground on a sandy road, and you'd hoped it would have

Picture referenced by Mr. Westbrook of second (foreground) and third county courthouses in downtown Burgaw. The current, or fourth, courthouse stands on the property in the background. *Courtesy of the Pender County Museum.*

rained the day before because then it wouldn't be quite so sandy because the sand was packed down at least in the ruts. We'd ride to Moore's Creek and back. At that time I believe the roads along Riley's Creek were paved, but many of these roads leading to places like Atkinson and Moore's Creek were not. They were still dirt. Yet we could be gone all day and Mom would not worry about us.

About downtown Burgaw, we'll start with the courthouse: that is the fourth courthouse for Pender County. The first one (I think) was in Willard. The second one was a clapboard siding building that sits where Laney [Real Estate] is now located, where First Citizens used to be. It was a little wooden-frame building with bars on the second floor: the jail was the second floor and the first floor was the court.

There's a picture of that building in the museum that shows the current courthouse property in the background. And I think it also shows the third courthouse that was built in the late 1800s.

Christmas parade in downtown Burgaw, 1957. *Courtesy of the Pender County Library.*

It was a brick structure but it was smaller than this. During the Works Progress Administration in the early 1930s, they dismantled that courthouse on this site and then utilized a lot of the parts—windows, doors and other things—and built what we have today. So it's the fourth courthouse.

The land itself is as large as it is because it was given by the railroad. When the railroad came through, they divided up the properties into roadways and...effectively four lots: four city blocks, a little over six acres in size. And that was donated. The railroad also donated land for a black school in the northern part of town and a white school in the southern part of town. And then it was graded off...so merchants bought the lots and started commerce. And it was all done around the railroad. And so the old depot that's here today—the first part of it—was built in the middle 1800s, maybe 1840...The part that is on the southern end, which is the most visibly attractive part, was a later addition and that was built in the early 1900s.

It was a real commerce center based on bringing your cotton and tobacco in, and anything that got shipped was shipped out of here. So people got used to coming here either once a week or once a month. There weren't that many cars, so they would come in on a horse and buggy. And then when they got cars, there were no big roads that connected to Wilmington, so they would still come here. Even during my lifetime this was an extremely active and vital retail center.

At Christmastime the sidewalks would be so full of people I can remember having to walk along the curb because you couldn't get by. You had your fine men's clothing next-door, Farrior's department store, with your hats from New York—the finest clothes you could buy. There were two drugstores, not just one. There was Dees' and also Durham's. There was Mr. Pullen's jewelry store, where everybody bought their diamonds. Every kind of little store that you could imagine you would want...

We even had a little movie house built by Senator Roy Rowe. And as I was growing up—again getting back to this sense of safety and security—I had been born overlooking the railroad tracks just around the corner on a lot that now has some apartments on it just down on Dickerson Street. It was a big Victorian house with winding porches on all four sides.

I can remember going to see *Abbott and Costello Meet Frankenstein*. And I must have been no older than five because the year I turned six we moved into the house that I live in today. And so I walked to that movie house at age five by myself and was so scared that I ran home because I couldn't sit through it when Frankenstein came up out of the coffin. It scared me, so I ran home. And I remember that. And, again, it wasn't that my mother was like, "Oh, I don't care about the kids." In fact, she was very protective. It's just the way it was back then. She was a very attentive mother. Daddy let Mother raise me because he was into his business. It was his job to make the money, and it was Mother's job to take care of the household. Of course, she worked right beside him. She was a nurse but right before she got a job as a nurse she had to make some money, and so she went to work for my daddy as a clerk in the store and ended up marrying him.

And the store was around the corner where my son is now in a place called Gramps Antiques and Collectibles. It's where my daddy started in 1936. So even then she worked right beside

Daddy and grew the business as I was growing up. But as a result I had a lot of freedom, and I took advantage of it. It was a wonderful time.

The jail was built in 1926, and it operated until 1972 and then sat vacant for about twenty-five years. The county was going to tear the building down and make a parking lot. Some of us became quite concerned. We had been meeting as a group of downtown merchants and had a little association called the Downtown Burgaw Association. So, we banded together and asked the county to give it to the town. The town didn't want it, so we said, "We'll take it." It was given to the Downtown Burgaw Association in 2000, and so we put a new roof on it, went in, cleaned up the inside and stabilized it. They have now leased it to a church group for a youth center.

The telephone company was where the Bank of America is now. The little house with the blue roof that's sitting next to it used to sit on the corner. [The owner of the telephone company] Mrs. Waddell knew where everybody was. If you wanted to find out where somebody was, you'd just call there and ask her, and she'd say, "No need to call them, they're not home." It really did work that way. She was into everybody's business because you had to call through and talk to an operator to get them to connect you with, say, Joe or Sam—and she would run it pretty much by herself. It was a very sociable time, and everybody knew everybody's business.

Totally Ivey:
Ivey Hayes

So often what you see is not about what you see.

Minutes before my interview with him ended, Ivey Hayes lifted his large paint-splattered hands and, dangling his long brown fingers forward, declared, "God's spirit is here!" Driving away, he raised a hand once more to wave goodbye. When he dropped it, all of nature seemed to fall in behind—sparrows, sunlight and soft breezes all looking to hitch a ride.

What little I'd known about this local painter was what I'd seen displayed in galleries around the lower Cape Fear area: surreal figures with long flowing bodies in bright colors with multiple folds that seemed to grow out of their surroundings—the farm, the jazz bar, the fishing pier. Whatever the subject, each canvas possessed the same cosmic vibration.

Born and raised on a farm outside Burgaw in an area known as Fennell Town, Ivey demonstrated an unusual gift for drawing and painting at an early age. Despite the lack of formal training in his youth, he went on to obtain a Master of Fine Arts degree from the University of North Carolina at Greensboro in 1975. His works have received national acclaim, including exhibition at the Capitol rotunda in Washington, D.C.

To experience Ivey is to occasion that rare artist who has transitioned from simply rendering his subject matter to finding himself in that subject matter. Recalling his father's farm and the annual county fair in Burgaw, Ivey spoke passionately of man's communion with nature, a relationship he has only recently come to understand completely.

> I was born in Pender County. As a child growing up, we lived on a farm and my dad was a farmer. But as a child growing up, I was given the gift of an artist, and it manifested itself at an early age. When I was in first grade, I don't ever remember drawing stick

figures. As a second grader I could outdraw my teachers. So the gift God had given me—which I didn't ask for, didn't plead for and didn't beg for—was given to me as a young child...

From there, the Lord just helped me to express myself artistically. I started painting in the third grade. I was painting complex and complicated compositions. I would paint stuff like birds, trees, the sky, buildings, grass and animals. Each year I became more acquainted with what I was doing, and I got better and better with drawing and painting.

At the same time I was still a farmer's kid. My dad was a very hard worker and my mom, too. Today, I can appreciate them more than ever before because it was hard growing up a farmer's kid. On weekends a lot of times we had to be in the field chopping or weeding. And so our childhood was a lot different from the lives of inner city kids. For us to go to the beach—and though we don't live too far from the beach—we were fortunate to go once a year. It was like a picnic, a tremendous celebration with a lot of food. To go to the beach once a year was a tremendous celebration.

My father's farm was off Fennell Town Road. The area was called Fennell Town because there were so many relatives of mine whose last name was Fennell. My mother's maiden name was Fennell. Keeping the farm going was really hard work. It was kind of like, "I'll be glad when this comes to an end." During school days when you'd come home after school, my dad always had chores for us to do. You'd get off the school bus, and he'd say, "All right, get out of those clothes and let's go to work." And so the only time we had to study was at night. Even though we were in school, when we got home, we had to go to work again.

But even though I thought one way then, when I think of what has happened to me as an adult, I realize now how blessed I was because in spite of the hardships we went through, in spite of the things we had to do, we never did go hungry because we had so much from the farm. We had cows, pigs, hogs and chickens. As far as crops we had watermelons, corn, peanuts, a variety of vegetables, beans and tomatoes. Our farm was about fifty acres. So much of the land we had to clear ourselves because it had trees on it. I tell people I'm a retired professional farm person!

In the family there were six boys and two girls. In the community everyone worked with everyone, and as far as the kids, we were subject to everyone in the community. The adults in the community were our angels. They watched over us, and if they told

Artwork with a rural American theme by Ivey Hayes. *Courtesy of Mr. Ivey Hayes.*

us something, we did it because the whole community raised each other, which is totally different from today. Back then you could sit on your porch and go to bed with your doors unlocked. These were things we cherished. Few people today have any idea what it's like to be loved by an entire community.

Each year we used to have the county fair here in Burgaw. And that was the number one thing as far as the schoolkids were concerned other than the state fair in Raleigh. You would save money, and money then was money! If you had a dollar in your pocket, you could ride forever. And so that was one of these things that as kids and adults we looked forward to year after year.

Some of the things you could see at the fair might be farm stuff like a huge hog. They'd try to show you the enormity of it. And then there was always the one part I enjoyed most about going: it was competition. They had first, second and third prizes when it came to things like sweet potatoes—you know, like who had the best-looking sweet potato. Sometimes they gave a description of how the vegetable was supposed to be presented, and so when it came to potatoes, watermelons, a variety of things, I would always enter because to win first prize was something like $2. Second prize was $1.50. Third prize was $1. But that was big money.

And so each year I would ask my dad if we could go into the field and find a huge watermelon. I would utilize the farm in instances like that in order to make money. However we could get money was a blessing from the Lord. I looked forward to it every year.

And then there was the artistic part—the best painting competition—so I would enter that, too. I would enter as many competitions as possible. Sometimes my mom would enter fruit preserves. So there was a variety of things that you could get into that involved a lot of the local people. It was fun, fun, fun! As far as my childhood, it was the number one event in Pender County.

The second event had to be the state fair. To go to the state fair was like, "Man, are you going to the state fair? Oh, man!" You rode on the activity bus and had to pay a certain amount of money, but it was fun. So if you were able to go to the county fair *and* state fair, it was a tremendous blessing from the Lord and your parents.

A lot of people wanted to go but couldn't go because their parents didn't have any money. For those who did go it was like cake and ice cream day. Today, for example, kids can go to the mall any day of the week, but the fair you planned for. This you saved your money for. And you would work and try to get money. You would start saving your money months before the fair because this was a way of life, an enjoyable part of life. Kids may go to the state fair today, but there's a tremendous difference in attitude.

Early in my art career I just tried to recreate what I was seeing in a natural way. I tried to copy or render them as I saw them. I didn't have an art teacher either in grade school or even high school. Growing up, I never had any formal training in the public school system. So when I would see the work of Pablo Picasso, I'd think, "Man, this guy has bumped his head, or he was just waiting for the people to come get him and put him in the white jacket." But, you see, that was due to ignorance. I didn't understand what was going on.

Only when I began to go to college did I begin to become aware of the importance of self-expression. But until then I only knew one thing, and that was to create what I could see visually. Anything that looked strange I thought the artist was trying to hide something or somebody had lost his mind. But that was due to ignorance because of my lack of knowledge.

More artwork by Ivey on display at the courthouse grounds during a festival. *Courtesy of Mr. Ivey Hayes.*

In life people mature. They change and get older. And life brings changes. You mature in the field you're in, and you don't stay the same. As a child I viewed things one way from a natural point of view. In college I began to view things a little bit differently because of being informed…I began to get into self-expression instead of just drawing and copying things from nature.

If you look at my work today, you'll see in my paintings that the bottoms tend to be flared out or very wavy. Now before that happened, before I accepted it…there wasn't anything I couldn't paint with watercolor. I could paint anything. When I got to that point, the Lord showed me that he was going to send me in another direction, and I didn't want to accept that. So for about five to six years I cried like a baby because I could no longer paint as I used to paint. My mind went blank. I couldn't remember how to do anything. Again I was trying to force myself to do a painting I couldn't do because I was being disobedient.

What you see today is what He was trying to get me to see back then, but I didn't want to accept it. When I did accept what He wanted me to do, then the whole world of color opened up. The flared out imagery was totally accepted. I call this "distorted perspective": it's like when you look at the Empire State Building, things get narrow as you look up. I'm not talking about true perspective. This is distorted perspective because in my paintings everything can be distorted or everything can be natural. When you look at the Empire State Building, you look up. Take that same point of view and throw it straight out, and that's what you see in my work.

So the things that you see in the painting today are not by accident—it's all due to where the Lord has been leading me. I am very happy about what I'm doing today. I'm very excited about the next painting. I wish I could live for a million years and I'm so excited because I have respect for even the grass. When I was painting watercolors in a natural way, all I was concerned about was trying to duplicate what I was seeing. But today I have a natural love for the grass, the leaves and insects. And whatever I paint, I become what I am painting. We become one and the same. I'm always on a journey. If I want to paint basketball players, even though I'm on crutches, I'm playing basketball. If I paint a fish, I become a fish. So often what you see is not about what you see.

Initially you would choose a way to paint that you know to be more satisfying, but the things you don't know can far exceed those you do know. You want to find out more about what you don't know, especially if it calls you to become more involved. And so with me today, you see a lot of my works that seem very colorful. Prior to this I began to get into color but not like it is today; it was more of the natural colors that I would use. But in college I would see people's work and be aware of different artists that would paint with color, so I began to color more than before, bright colors or secondary or third colors.

Here again today I'm growing. I'm a student. I'm seeing things and I'm experiencing things, which is normal. Before I really learned to put myself into the paintings, I wasn't satisfied. I was always self-motivated, and so I didn't need someone to say, "Ivey, you ought to try this." I was constantly trying to improve and express myself. But I had a problem, and the problem was when it came to self-expression, I was more involved with people I loved seeing, and I would filter that into things I was drawing.

I wasn't really "Ivey." I was just a part of "Ivey" and part of so many other people. But today I'm totally "Ivey," and that's the difference.

Grab Your Sea Bag:
Horace S. Lefler

By that time, the stench was so awful that you could smell it twenty miles out to sea.

More than sixty years later, Horace Lefler's ebullient voice still hinted at the young adventure-seeking farm boy who worked and roamed the Pender countryside on the eve of World War II.

Like most boys his age—sixteen, seventeen and eighteen—tobacco picking had become tiresome and the sandy grit of eastern North Carolina soil all too familiar. For Horace and countless others, military service meant three squares a day, a steady paycheck and a giant leap from fieldstone to Europe's cobblestone that seemed special made for American boys in search of destiny.

I first heard him mentioned by Mary Caputo, whose museum tour included personal possessions from Pender residents who fought in the war. With his cover tilted far back on his head, an airman in one portrait gazed undaunted at the sky. War or no war, he looked happy to have found himself behind a one-thousand-horsepower engine at thirty thousand feet. Rouge on the cheeks of a young army nurse in another picture seemed so heavily applied it looked like the picture had been snapped yesterday.

Mr. Lefler was interviewed several years back by Mr. Lee Johnson, who compiled recollections of World War II veterans in Pender County. His interviews were transcribed by the Pender County Historical Society and are currently on file at the state archives in Raleigh. In speaking with Mr. Lefler over the phone recently, I formed the youthful composite of an eager young man with neatly combed hair, polished shoes and a starched uniform. During both my own conversation with Mr. Lefler and the interview with Mr. Johnson, in my mind spotlights searched, flak exploded and big band names like Glenn Miller and Tommy Dorsey flashed, as Horace revealed details of boot camp at Parris Island and the horrors that awaited him at Iwo Jima in February 1945.

I was born in Cabarrus County in 1924. We left there and moved to the coastal plain when I was approximately five years old, and I lived here, mostly in Pender County. I went to high school at Penderlea and graduated from there in 1943. From there I joined the Marine Corps. I went to Parris Island on May 26. I was there from May until around sometime in October: three or four months at Parris Island at boot camp. When I finished boot camp, my first assignment was Washington, D.C., at the Marine Barracks headquarters. I stayed there for three, four, five months as an honor guard for dignitaries and parades and that kind of stuff. It was spit and polish—practice marching…It was an experience. For the time there I enjoyed it, but you get tired of the spit and polish. One day they came around and told me I was getting transferred, and I said, "Where?" and they said, "You will know when you get there."

That was in the fall of '43. And they loaded me on a truck with my sea bag and off we went. We wound up on the top of the mountains at Camp Shangri-La. That was President Roosevelt's hideaway during World War II. (It's Camp David now. Eisenhower renamed it after his grandson.) Anyway, I was up at the camp with Roosevelt until the summer of '44. Roosevelt was in very bad shape at the time. Of course, you know that he was in a wheelchair. He couldn't be by himself, so [for] anything that he had to participate in, he had to be moved and propped up. He couldn't stand up, so we had a prop that he sat on. Anyway, he was getting [to be] in very poor health.

We didn't have direct contact with him. One time he ate dinner with us. There were about sixty Marines in this detail, and I don't know how many Secret Service. We worked under them. They had direct contact with him, and we were the backup: outer perimeter security. I did see him a lot. I spoke with Mrs. Roosevelt quite a few times. And anyway, in the summer of '44, he got real bad off, and they were going to take him to Warm Springs, Georgia. And they didn't think he would ever come back to Camp Shangri-La. So we were busted up; part of us went to Georgia, and the other part was sent out to the Marine Corps. So I ended up at Camp Lejeune for some advance training, which I had never had because I had left boot camp to go straight into Washington.

Roster of Pender County veterans of World War II. *Courtesy of Pender County Library.*

So they sent me to Camp Lejeune for a couple of months, and then in October they transferred me to Camp Pendleton for a few days, and then after that they loaded a transport full of replacements and sent us to Maui and Hawaii to join the Twenty-third Marines. They were practicing for the Iwo-Okinawa invasion. I trained with the Twenty-third Marines, Second Battalion. In December a few days before Christmas, they loaded us on transports and LSVs (or Logistics Support Vessels) and we went to sea for landing maneuvers. So some time in the first part of February, we wound up in Saipan for a few days. We unloaded a few transports on to LSVs. The landing crews were the ones that were going to make the initial landing. After we left Saipan, they told us where we were going: a little island not too far away by the name of Iwo Jima, which none of us had ever heard of.

We had lessons on what the island was like and what they were projecting it was going to be like. We were to take Iwo in seventy-two hours. They indicated it would be just another training mission, and we boarded the ships and proceeded. We'd pick up more troops and had the Fifth Marine Division with us, the Fourth Marine Division and the Third Marine Division and probably some units I never knew. Anyway, we were to proceed after Iwo to Okinawa. And we would be projected to be back aboard ship in seventy-two hours or less. Well, when we got there, we had schooling on the islands. They had mock-ups of the defenses, of what we would see. The place had been bombed for about sixty days by the navy and the air force.

When we landed on February 19, I was supposed to be in the second wave of units. In the first wave, the Fifth Division was over to our left. They were to go in, and one outfit was to swing left and take Mount Suribachi, and the other was to cut across and swing east to the other side of the island. We were the Fourth Division and were supposed to go straight in and take the airfield, which was in operation. Then the Third Division sent in a whole regiment to the right of us. They were to go in and turn right. All three units were to swing to the right and go to the end of the island, which was about five miles long.

Well, we were going in, and everything was peaceful and quiet. The first wave was supposed to have been a wave of amphibious tanks to clear the way on the beach. Well, the first wave got mixed up, and then we all landed about the same time at about eight minutes after eight on February 19. Our objective was every man in every unit in the front was to advance toward the airfield. The airfield was three to four hundred yards inland. And of course, the island was not level; it had hills. And the airfield was built up. Along the ocean side of the airfield was a big bank. So we organized on the beach on that big bank, which was about thirty feet high. Anyway, when we landed going into the beach, we took a little fire, just some shell once in a while. Of course, it didn't take us long to get from the landing craft to the beach.

We hit the beach, and it was quiet. Nothing going on. We disembarked and got organized and started inland. We got in—I guess about 175 yards, maybe 200. We had everything organized to make the initial push toward the airfield. And all of a sudden that whole island started. The shells came in waves, like raindrops. It was soft sand. You would mire up to your knees in this black volcanic ash. It wasn't nice sand; it was more like granulated black sand. And the Japanese started to fire—it was just like the whole island exploded. So the only thing we could do was to get back down. We couldn't dig a foxhole. If you tried to dig in the sand, it would just cover you up. Which was a good thing because that black loose sand saved a lot of lives. When those shells started landing, they would go deep. When the explosives went off, the shrapnel had a tendency to dive rather than spray. Therefore, [the sand buried the shrapnel and] saved a lot of lives.

The Japanese had their artillery aimed at just a certain spot—just one square. Therefore, they had the whole island covered. After they started firing, there was nothing we could do but stay down. Me and a couple of other fellows got into a shell hole and got up on the rim of it and squished down in the sand. And we stayed there. We couldn't fire a rifle because we couldn't see anybody. We stayed there from 8:30 in the morning until dark. We couldn't move; they had us pinned down. There were a lot of pillboxes between the airfield and us. You couldn't stand up. The best you could do was look over the rim of that shell hole.

Of course, we did fire some. When it got dark, we started to try to re-form and get our lines straightened out, and when you went from one hole to another, you wouldn't find anybody but dead people. If there were five in a hole, maybe one would be alive. It was that way up and down the beach. So finally, about an hour after dark, me and the fellows that had been in that shell hole all day together started looking, trying to get men together for the night.

[By] about ten o'clock, we [found] about sixty-five to seventy men. We had a very, very high casualty rate that first day. Fortunately, the next morning we got organized and started the push to the part of the island near the airfield. But there was supposed to have been a rendezvous within an hour or an hour and a half that first day. Well, it took us three days to get to the rendezvous point by the airfield. We finally got there and lunch was being served.

We had to have replacements; I don't know how many replacements we got, but we lost (I would say) a third of the men out of the companies that were first on the beach. We organized there under the airfield on the third day, and we tried to take the airfield. We'd stab at it and get pushed back. We'd stab at it again and get pushed back. The rest of the lines were suffering the same way we were. We just couldn't move. The Fifth Division on the left had split. One unit was to take Mount Suribachi. They couldn't. They were deep down. They were suffering tremendous casualties, and the other group was supposed to cut straight across, cut that volcano and separate it from the other island. They couldn't move.

So it was just back and forth, back and forth, for—I don't know—it seemed like a week. It was [actually] three or four days.

Finally, they took Mount Suribachi and about the third or fourth day we looked up and saw a flag on top, so the Fifth had gotten up there. But it wasn't the publicity flag that we put up later. There was a flag, but in a couple of days they took it down and raised the famous one.

We looked up and saw that flag and said, "Well, we're here anyway. We're going to stay." Like I said, it was a seesaw. The loss of men and the casualty rate was just staggering. You couldn't expose yourself because the whole east end of the island was cliffs and caves and stuff. They would have their big guns, roll them out and fire four or five rounds. And before the ships out at sea could get a lock on them, they would stop and roll them back in the caves. The big guns were on railroad tracks, and they would roll them back and forth.

Anyway, we finally took that first airfield and turned toward the second airfield that was under construction. They had just bulldozed it up. Like I said, some days we wouldn't move at all. Some days we'd move fifty yards and then move back twenty-five. Lots of days you wouldn't see any Japanese. But if you stuck your head up, they would try to shoot it off. You couldn't organize a push because there was so much fire. In fact, we were pinned down in a foxhole most of the time. But then we would make a stab at moving. Sometimes we might move twenty-five yards. Sometimes we might get fifty yards. Fifty yards would be a big gain. Of course, all the time we were losing men.

Then we started drawing replacements from the other regiments. It seemed like we could never gain back the strength. We just didn't have enough replacements for that whole operation, but we got some. We just spent day after day (more or less) in hand-to-hand combat. We were never much over a hundred yards from the enemy and of course they had the high ground. They were dug in pillboxes and blockhouses and caves. We'd call for fire on those blockhouses. Out at sea we had the battleships and cruisers firing almost constantly. They were the battleships with the sixteen-inch guns.

After we got on the island and fought our way across, we called for floating artillery ships out at sea: cruisers, destroyers and battleships. Some of the blockhouses would have walls of six- to eight-feet-thick concrete-reinforced steel. And I have seen a sixteen-inch shell hit one of them, plow through and rise up again and skid across the island. It never did explode. And the ones that were going over, we could stick our hand up with a match and strike it as that sixteen-inch shell went over. There was just a continuous roll of gunfire—big stuff. And in turn we were facing the little stuff, which would kill you just as dead as the big stuff. But we would inch forward…In the meantime we were losing men, more than we could get replaced. And the lines were getting thinner and thinner, and we moved halfway across the island in about fifteen days, I guess it was. Like I say, it was inch by inch and foot by foot. If we did make a gain, the terrain was so full of caves we'd move up fifty yards, and the next morning we would have Japanese fifty yards behind us.

The turning point came about the seventeenth or eighteenth day. We had taken one of the hills that had been giving us so much trouble. We had taken it so the observation teams could tell the rest of the island where the true concentration was. But you see the ground that we took was full of caves. We would seal them up the best we could. Tanks weren't much use on the island because they couldn't get over certain terrain that we had to fight in. So they converted a lot of them into flamethrowers. The barrels of the guns were fitted with some kind of lining, I don't know. And they would bring the tanks up on those caves, and if we could get to the pillboxes and blockhouses, we would get a flamethrower up there. The heat would be so intense that—when we looked in there after we passed it—that napalm was just burning so bad like a cookie, like a hot dog. We just kept punching and punching and falling back and punching until we finally got things so we could move.

And, of course, all the time it was just hand-to-hand combat. This went on for fifteen to eighteen days, and we could see that we were really getting into the high ground, so we finally got a little bit of an advantage. But we just had to keep plugging, and on about the eighteenth day we got word that there would be no more replacements. So we had to finish it. But the thing was we had plenty overhead fire from the planes, we had fire from the ships, so it was just one continuous war of shells and mortar and artillery and small arms, and of course we found out that the whole island was almost hollow. In the big caves, they had warehouses behind the ground. You would dig a foxhole at night, and you could hear noise [and] vibrations under you. Moving equipment and stuff. The saying was that you don't dig a foxhole very deep because you might fall through. It was an awful thing. We spent twenty-six days, and we didn't get any relief. We had to stay on the line, and it was constant, constant fire for twenty-six days.

You got rest. You could dig in the best you could at night. If you had a partner, you would get a little nap. But, of course, you didn't always have someone with you in the foxhole, as there weren't that many men. If you had a partner, you would sleep an hour, and he would sleep an hour. Of course, we were always subject to a night attack. We stayed on the defensive at night. The Japanese once in a while would pull a little attack. If we could hook them we could get them to pull a charge. The first one they pulled was the eighth of March.

At about five o'clock in the morning they started a-whooping and a-howling and coming at us, and of course we were waiting for them. And the next morning we had a pile of Japanese in front of our foxhole—you could hardly see over them. I think the count was three or four hundred men that we had in front of us. After that we punched our way on to the twenty-sixth of March. We could see the water on the other side. They relieved us, and we came back for a day. On the way back there were so many dead Japanese—of course, [the Japanese] did not recover any of their dead—and the Marines did a good job of removing the casualties. There were so many dead that we had to clean up our section going back. We just disposed of the bodies in the shell holes and had a bulldozer come along to cover them up. By that time, the stench was so awful that you could smell it twenty miles out to sea—between the bodies that had not been taken care of and the sulphur. The Japanese had a lot of gunpowder made from sulphur. Also, there were some sulphur pits on the island. Between all of that the stench was so bad you could hardly stand it. Anyway, they relieved us on the twenty-sixth of March and brought us back, and we boarded ship somewhere four to five days later. We didn't go on to Okinawa—we were shot up so bad—that they sent us back to our training base, which was Maui in the Hawaii group. Then we started training for Japan.

Courtesy of Horace S. Lefler Papers, Military Collection, Archives and Records Section, North Carolina Office of Archives and History, Raleigh.

The Mystery of Place: Evelyn Bradshaw

So she kept hemming and hawing and said, "It isn't much." And I said, "I don't care. Let's go."

A mid a sea of people lunching, handshaking and chatting, I turned to see an unexpected portrait of a woman with glasses and a windswept scarf in a quiet corner of the Topsail Island Assembly Building. Against painted gray cinder blocks, pictures of bow-tied men holding metal gadgets and a life-size missile (dead, of course), her whimsical grin put the room at ease. With its brown, bronze and amber hues and earthy texture, the picture and its subject looked like they'd made a wrong turn, forsaking warm sands and a crystal coast just a couple hundred yards east for the building that once supported the U.S. Navy's fledgling missile program.

When I met Evelyn Bradshaw, the woman in the portrait, in her Hampstead home, the feeling of sunlight and sand between the toes returned. A native of Washington, North Carolina, Evelyn had come to live in Wilmington, where she learned of Topsail Island, a forty-minute drive north, over a game of bridge.

In the years between 1946 and 1948, the United States government and military established its ramjet missile test site on land that it had claimed on Topsail, effectively launching the country's jet age. According to official literature, dozens of the nation's top scientists converged on the assembly building (which now houses the Missles and More Museum) and built over two hundred experimental rockets, ranging in length from three to thirteen feet. Rumors persist the top-secret program employed German scientists who had conceived the V-2 assault rocket. Another rumor lays claim to a secret tunnel underneath the facility.

As we sat in her sunroom on an unusually cool spring day, laughing and wishing for warmer weather, Evelyn described watching her kids grow up on the island, how she became involved in the Historical Society of Topsail Island, the acquisition of the assembly building and the mystique of Operation Bumblebee.

I first went to the island in 1961 through Jane Watson, who was a member of the Bland family. Her grandfather had a mile of property from the ocean to the sound right in Topsail Beach (part of it was in Surf City, actually). And I had played bridge with Jane in Wilmington, and she said something about going up to Topsail Island to a cabin, and of course I perked right up and said, "You have a cabin at the beach?"

I had never been to Topsail Island. My husband had been there to do some beach erosion studies, so I was aware of it. So she kept hemming and hawing and said, "It isn't much." And I said, "I don't care. Let's go." So we made plans to go, and I said, "We'll go up there and play bridge, and we'll take our kids and play all day and stay the night." Well, she was still a little embarrassed about the whole thing.

When we got there, the cabin was just inside Topsail Beach, just after you leave Surf City, on the sound. It was a fishing shack; it had no bathroom. It did have electricity but no running water—it had a pump…When we got there, we parked on the road and had to walk. You couldn't drive down to it. It wasn't very far but I had to take a crib. I had a baby. Brad was not even a year old.

The cabin was just a shack. It was one room that had been partitioned with curtains with a bunch of bunk beds behind the curtains and a kitchen that had a cookstove (probably gas) and a sink and no running water. You had to bring the water in, and the pump was right out in front of the house. There was a bathtub: a claw-foot bathtub. You took that bathtub and what you did was pump the water in there—they had to prime the pump to get it started—and pump that thing full of water and let it sit in the sun and heat it. Then everyone would bathe in it.

We took all the kids to the beach. Now I had four children, Jane had three children, Ruth Edwards had two of her three and Ruth Coleman had her two children. There were plenty of bunks. I mean they had bunks everywhere, stacked like layers—three stacks. We played all day on that ocean and then came home and cooked and ate and fed all of the kids. They were so tired, but first we bathed them in that tub of water. First they rinsed off all the salt and sand, and then the adults got in and bathed in it. "Oh Lord, help us," we'd say.

Then we got the kids all settled down and everybody was worn out, but, man, we were primed to play bridge and we played bridge all night long. They had a little tiny grocery store right up the road from us. It was called the Cracker Box. It's not there anymore—hasn't been there since one of the storms. The owner just sold bread and had some milk. I guess it was refrigerated milk. I don't know if he had refrigeration or not, but mostly it was crackers, and they called it the Cracker Box. Jane's cousin ran it, so we sat up and played bridge all night. We did this two or three times. We'd go up, spend the night and just play bridge. But that was my introduction to the island.

There was nothing for as far as you could look. The shack was right by the Gold Hole…That's where the prospectors were looking for gold. Everybody threw everything into the hole. I mean there were chairs, anything—whole iceboxes. You couldn't see to the bottom. There was water in the bottom. You'd throw things down there, and there were snakes down there too. I mean fierce ones—copperheads and rattlesnakes. None of the adults would go up there to throw the trash away. We would make the kids go three or four at a time and run up there and throw it in and run down, and no self-respecting snake would come near them. And that is how we got rid of our trash.

But my children almost cried when the shack burned some years later. We graduated to being able to rent some places. First we rented and shared with another couple and their children. But then we got so we rented our own place, but we always managed to get there with the other family and have our vacations together. These kids grew up together.

When we bought a place at Topsail in 1973, I still didn't know much about the island's history, until one night someone asked me to go to a historical society meeting. I didn't even know they had a society. And I have always been a history buff anyway, so I thought it would be fun. I got there, and they didn't have a speaker. There were six people there. It was about to fold. They had to elect officers that night and out of the six they couldn't get enough volunteers to get enough officers. Finally, I said, "You know something, if you'll let me go home, I'll be the secretary." I said, "I am so tired, I have got to go home."

The Mystery of Place: Evelyn Bradshaw

Fun at Topsail Beach on the Pender County coast. *Courtesy of Topsail Historic Society.*

By that time my children were older and weren't home much. They were in college, and I think I only had one at home at that time. So I started in with the historical society, and I got in with Betty Polzer. She was from New Jersey, but she was so interested in the history there, and she did a lot towards acquiring the assembly building and getting all that publicized, so everyone knew what value there was in the building. She died about ten years ago, I guess. But she got involved in it, and we finally decided if we couldn't meet at night and attract new people, we'd meet for lunch—we could go to a restaurant. Everybody loves to eat out.

So we did and our membership kept increasing. And then we started getting speakers, and in the meantime there was all this interest about getting a museum. Betty had encouraged the Topsail Beach Economic Development Council, which was a nonprofit organization, to buy the assembly building. It was for sale, and it was in danger of being torn down. It's where the rockets were assembled, so it was very important historically.

I had moved up from vice-president to president of the Historical Society at that time, which I had never intended to do. I had a treasurer who was really gung-ho on doing something, and I said,

Facility Observation Tower #2 on Topsail Island built in support of the U.S. Navy's top-secret missile-testing program, Operation Bumblebee, 1946–48. *Courtesy of Topsail Historic Society.*

"Look, let's open the assembly building and see what happens. What difference does it make? We've got the building. All we have to do is take a few pictures, hang them up and see what happens." Our treasurer said we had $600, so I said, "We'll work until the $600 is gone and then we'll quit." So we opened the thing and David Stalman got us all these pictures from Johns Hopkins—they partnered with the Navy Ordnance to build the testing site…We hung those up. It was going to be about Operation Bumblebee, and finally I found out about Operation Bumblebee and what the towers were for. I started reading up on it and said, "You know, this really pretty neat" and got really interested in it. You wouldn't believe how successful we were that first summer. There were people who brought their children down to learn about those towers and about Operation Bumblebee.

No one was allowed on the island between 1946 and 1948 during Operation Bumblebee. It was closed off. About once a year they would allow property owners on the island, but even then they couldn't go to the south end of the island where the assembly building was. The rockets were assembled inside the building and the towers were strategically located all the way up to the north end of the island. Tower one was on the south end, and the rockets were fired east and slightly north and all the towers had people with equipment in there.

The Mystery of Place: Evelyn Bradshaw

There are stories about a tunnel. There may have been a utility tunnel; I'm not sure. I've got two people who swear they played in it and that it was a great big room. One of them said they had furniture down there. And they may have. I think there might have been some kind of utility, but when Hurricane Hazel hit in 1954 there was sand everywhere and there's a theory that if there had been any kind of tunnel for utilities it was probably covered up with sand. But there are people who swear there was a tunnel.

There's lots more little stories about Operation Bumblebee, of course. At that time the United States was utilizing German scientists—Wernher von Braun had been the biggie in Germany. He had helped develop their rocket program. When it came time that the United States got to Germany before the end of the war, there was a point, I understand, when von Braun had a choice—either go to the Russians or come to us—he came to us. He turned over trainloads (about five cars' worth) of research information to us. In the process, they got him to the United States along with a bunch of other German scientists, and they went to Huntsville, Alabama. And at one time they said German was spoken more in Huntsville in that research station than English.

I can't believe von Braun would be in Huntsville and not wonder what was going on up at Topsail and come up here. There was one interview with a man on the mainland who worked over here during that time, and he was totally in the dark to what it was, but he said on the north side of the assembly building there was a compound type of thing and that the people in there weren't exactly prisoners but they weren't exactly free to roam a whole lot. I just have a feeling there had to be a few Germans here. The head of the program was Tad Stanwick—he was the naval commander heading up the program. I never could get him to agree to an interview. I asked him a while ago, "Tad, why won't you tell me all this stuff?" He said, "Actually, I'm sworn to secrecy for three more years."

Epilogue

As fresh eyes fall upon these pages to edit in preparation for first printing, the people of Pender County will have enjoyed another successful Spring Fest on the courthouse square. And they will be hard at work finalizing last-minute details for June's North Carolina Blueberry Festival.

They will have seen April's azaleas bloom and suffered May's one or two ninety-degree days—a primer to the infernos of July and August when window units on store sides sag and sweat from their Sisyphean task.

On these insufferable summer days, men will trickle into Ray's barbershop and talk about the price of gas and milk, how they suspect the harvest will do and who they think will be the next president. Shopkeepers along Wright Street will slowly sweep the sidewalk, as passersby window-shop. At the lunch counter at Dees' Drugstore, people will line up for cool fresh-squeezed lemonade and homemade pimento cheese sandwiches. During a recess at the courthouse, men and women will file out of the brick and concrete edifice to make a phone call or grab a smoke.

One of these people will no doubt gaze off into the distance, noting how the sunlight hits a tree a certain way, how a park bench frames a family sharing a picnic, how an old picture that slips from a wallet requires a second look. Emotions that follow next are like cupcakes to the brain—the fanciful, endorphin-charged flight back to an earlier place and time.

Then, like a slow-motion camera, the mind's eye will begin to recreate the scene and for a split second—the time it takes for a sip of lemonade or a single sweep of the broom—we can have access to ourselves as we once were. Our breathing will slow. Our shoulders may slump. We may laugh at our old selves, shake our heads and dismiss ourselves, maybe even well up in tears at ourselves. Whatever we do, we rarely come away unaffected.

This is the nature of history.

What sustains the history of a place like Pender County—indeed, any place—is not only its centuries-old structures and noteworthy events but also its residents' ability to identify with their personal connection to the area.

In these remarkable stories you find storytellers constantly in pursuit of themselves, willing to examine who they are, where they've come from and where they're going.

Visit us at
www.historypress.net

www.ingramcontent.com/pod-product-compliance
Lightning Source LLC
Chambersburg PA
CBHW060755100426
42813CB00004B/820